AUTOGRAPH

DREAM BIG
START SMALL

AWAKEN THE ENTREPRENEUR WITHIN

• •

*Learn how to find your passion, build a brand around it,
and get paid doing what makes you happy!*

EL PASO, TEXAS

Copyrighted Material

Dream Big Start Small

Copyright © 2023 by Dr. Mikel Brown. All Rights Reserved.

No part of this publication may be reproduced, stored in retrieval system or transmitted, in any form or by any means electronic, mechanical, photocopying, recording, or otherwise without prior written permission from the publisher, except for the inclusion of brief quotations in a review.

Unless otherwise indicated, all scripture quotations are taken from the New International Version of the Bible.

For information about this title or to order other books and/or electronic media, contact the publisher:

CJC Publishing Company
1208 Sumac Drive, El Paso, Texas 79925
www.cjcpublishing.com

Library of Congress Control Number: 2023935123

ISBN: 978-1-930388-24-6

Printed in the United States of America.

Cover and Interior design by CJC Publishing Company.

TABLE OF CONTENTS

Dedication vi

Introduction viii

1 The Enemy of 'NOW' 1

2 The Importance of Financial Literacy 9

3 The Cost to Be a Boss 17

4 Starting a Small Business 25

5 Increase Your Net Worth Through Multiple Streams of Income 31

6 Ten Creative Business Ideas You Can Start 39

7 Step by Step 47

8 The Energy Derived From Disciplined Thinking 57

9 Transform your Money Mindset 63

10 Money Doesn't Promote You, Your Thinking Does 69

11	A Business Affair	77
12	Pregnant With a Dream	83
13	Five Distinctive Rules to Propel Your Business	89
14	Seize The Moment	95
15	Wings of Your Imagination	107
16	Don't Sell Yourself Short by Being Average	117
17	The Gospel of Entrepreneurship and Creating Wealth	125
18	Why Should You Own Land And Properties	137
	About The Author	143

DEDICATION

I dedicate this book to God Almighty my creator, my strong pillar, my source of inspiration, wisdom, knowledge and understanding. Jesus the Christ has been the source of my strength throughout my life and on His wings only, have I soared.

I also devote this work to my wife and all six of my children, their spouses, grandchildren and great grandchildren. Also, to my mother who gave birth to me and my brothers. In loving memory of my brother, Jeff Jr.

I would be remiss not to include a very warm heartfelt thanks, with genuine gratitude and warm regard, to a young man who embraced my words like a good son, without compensation. Mr. Charles, you'll never know how I appreciate your diligence and desire to serve.

To my staff who work so hard to ensure that my vision

DEDICATION

comes to pass, and who goes beyond the call of duty, I say just because…

Thank you to all! My love for all of you can never be quantified. God bless you!

INTRODUCTION

Before you find yourself uber driving or Door Dashing someone's dinner to their doorstep for extra cash, please pay attention to what I have to say! Seriously, it'll change your life!

I have never seen anyone get rich from working an ordinary 9 to 5 job, or as I like to refer to it, a J.O.B (just over broke). It is not as if people cannot become wealthy and create more income; they just lack the knowledge of how to do so. In essence, what you don't know can keep you poor. The acronym for 'poor' is passing over opportunities repeatedly. When you're living paycheck to paycheck, often your mindset is not geared towards ways to elevate your income. For some, being tired of living from paycheck to paycheck can be the catalyst to making the necessary changes to become wealthy.

I know how frustrating it can be when you have more

INTRODUCTION

month at the end of your money than money at the end of your month. With these frustrations comes the belief that you must hold on tight to the little that you have and make it last. People generally believe the only way to increase their income is through a pay raise or a second job. They need clarification and support about creative ways to increase their income. Although an extra job may be viable for some, alternatives are available for increasing one's income without overextending oneself or adding to the stress load. On top of that, most employers are not handing out raises to the average employee; instead, they are spreading the wealth among their top Executives.

Let's face it; working yourself to death is not the answer to increasing your income. And, even if you were successful at increasing your income by working extremely hard or having two jobs, you probably will only be around for a short while to enjoy it. There are two guaranteed ways to increase your income. You chase your money until you have caught up with it, which makes you work harder, or you can learn how to attract money and make it work for you, and in so doing, work smarter.

YOU MAKE THE CHOICE. GET A JOB OR CREATE ONE.

There is a powerful scripture in the Bible that, if believed, can be an unequivocal booster for one's self-confidence. This verse has empowered me to create opportunities that multiply my earnings by producing income streams. This Bible verse does not pacify the self-

INTRODUCTION

helpless person. It places the ball in the individual's court to deliver actionable results to improve their income. For me, this is a self-help verse.

> Deuteronomy 8:18 NIV But remember the LORD your God, for it is he who gives you the ability to produce wealth...

Hundreds of millions of people have subliminally given credit for the ability to make money on some special gift that only a select few have. Therefore, the person who believes this philosophy to be accurate has already accepted their nominal salary and inserted themselves in the average and ungifted category. This philosophy couldn't be further from the truth. Whether or not people believe in their intrinsic ability to make as much money as they want to, based on this Bible verse, God has given every human the gift and right to create or produce wealth.

Playing dumb is not going to better your situation, and sticking your head in the sand to avoid the obvious, isn't going to make your financial woes disappear. People who think they have money problems are sadly mistaken; their actual problem is not money; it is the lack of information and belief in their God-given ability to create wealth. To stop this infectious supposition from permeating the next generation, parents have a responsibility to instruct their children and embed in their psyche that they have an inherent ability to make and manage money. Hence, they will already be ahead of the money-making curve when they become young adults.

INTRODUCTION

I want to change how millions of people worldwide think about producing and increasing wealth. Some viewpoints often contradict and challenge conventional wisdom; mine is one of them. The first step for income multiplication is to believe that income multiplication is possible. Go ahead and take the first step. Then the invisible will come into view.

CHAPTER ONE

THE ENEMY OF 'NOW'

The two most important days of your life are the day that you were born, and the day that you find out why.
~ Dr. Mikel A Brown

. . . .

CHAPTER ONE

THE ENEMY OF 'NOW'

WHICH WOULD YOU CHOOSE, start a business and help others, or continue to be mediocre and spend your time doing unimportant things while living someone else's dream? You will never regret making the right choice. Just get started; I promise you will love where your business takes you.

Just think about all the things that could happen. Consider the possibility of increasing your income, supplying financial support for your family and church, and having more time for yourself. All those things are worth investing in yourself. The key to success is being intentional. Get started on your business project now and take the proper steps that will help you reach your goals faster.

Procrastination is the most common form of self-sabotage and producer of performance anxiety. The good news is that it is entirely preventable. Continue reading this book to learn how to make the right choice, perform all things necessary to start a business, and get more done with less stress.

The Enemy Of 'NOW"

There is one word every procrastinator is afraid of hearing, and that word is "NOW." A procrastinator loves to say, "Let me sleep on it," or "I'm going to pray about it." However, all a procrastinator does is sleep and call it prayer.

So many of us put things off, not because we're always indecisive or lazy, but because deep down inside all of us is a perfectionist who fears failure. Our inner perfectionist wants the ideal conditions to exist before they start. They want the perfect outcome. What they want to do is succeed without failing. However, most experts will tell you that the only way to true success is through many failures. How many times does a baby fall on their bottom before they walk? If they gave up after that first time or never tried for fear of falling, we'd have a society of crawlers!

Have you ever noticed the perseverance of a baby who wants to walk? They are uncompromising in their efforts. It's when they become older that they become fearful of challenges. Fear is a learned behavior. We are taught by our parents, friends, movies and books what to be afraid of confronting.

So, what do you want to start or need to begin but your inner perfectionist keeps telling you to put off? Perfection, often, is a need for everything to be "just right", which can be a cover-up for the fears that exist within the person. Show me a man who waits for opportunities, and I will show you a poor man.

People are always saying that they are tired of living from paycheck to paycheck, but they are usually too tired to do something about it. Procrastination will always make you the victim; action will unequivocally make you the victor. Your most significant deterrent in starting a business or experiencing victory in any given area is your inability to remain focused on the chief aspects that will allow you to walk in success. Distraction has won the battle for your focus if you can easily be pulled away from what you are doing.

You will be surprised at what a plan will do for you, despite how brief it may be. Your plan can be as simple as:

- Get up early, sign up for classes, or read a Bible chapter.

- Clean the closet, straighten the garage, and search for a new house.

- Write one page of your book, go to a local bookstore to look for books on starting a business, or buy Dr. Brown's book, "UNEXPECTED TREASURES"...

People complicate things when life can be pretty straightforward. To not plan your life means you have scheduled nothing, in particular, to happen in your life. So why aren't most people going for the gusto? People never plan to be failures; they fail to plan to be successful. The lazier the man, the more he plans to do tomorrow. Therefore, a good plan today is better than a perfect plan tomorrow. If planning is a formula for success, then a life without planning is a recipe for disaster.

Solomon urged his readers not to sit around waiting for the most opportune moment to work but to be diligent constantly. Controlling every situation is not in your power, but deciding how you respond to those situations is in your power. So, waiting for the right moment to do something significant will result in inactivity.

The Enemy Of 'NOW'

Ecclesiastes 11:4 "Whoever watches the wind will not plant; whoever looks at the clouds will not reap."

Ecclesiastes 11:6 "Sow your seed in the morning, and at evening let not your hands be idle, for you do not know which will succeed, whether this or that, or whether both will do equally well."

The most common reality in business is that waiting on the best deal frequently causes the procrastinator to pick through the crumbs of the one who moved first. What you could pay less for NOW will cost you more in the long run. It is always economically beneficial to decide now rather than later. Is your hesitance destroying you or serving you? Is it helpful or harmful to your life? Operating in uncertainty or indecisiveness is nothing more than making a bold move toward standing still.

You must have a sense of urgency when God speaks or when you have an intuition about something. I have learned that God has all the time in the world, but I don't. Time is my enemy if I procrastinate but it is my ally if I move or persist. Activity is the key to God blessing you.

Proverbs 10:4 "Lazy hands make a man poor, but diligent hands bring wealth."

Proverbs 12:24 "Diligent hands will rule (govern), but laziness ends in slave labor."

People who do nothing with their dreams are just as guilty of being faithless as people who only talk about them. If you are an alum of Average State University, your degree can only be in Mediocrity. Mediocrity is excellent in the eyes of mediocre people. Sometimes our minds become contaminated with things that may not kill us but can get us sick. You get food poisoning from eating the wrong spiritual and mental foods (negativity).

Friends, your future is in danger if you live a mediocre existence. The ten men who spied out the Promised Land said (nevertheless), or in our modern language, they said, 'but'. As soon as I see that (but), I know trouble is brewing. This one little word has robbed more people of their faith, stolen their health, robbed them of their dreams, kept them from their miracle and slammed the door shut to the promises of God.

How often have we stood on the border of our Promised Land and failed to take possession? Every time you add a (but) to the things you would like to carry out, you limit the God in you from working and imprison yourself. You are disqualifying yourself from God's promises, His provision, and His ability to work through you.

When God told Moses about the Promised Land flowing with milk and honey, houses they wouldn't have to build, or land that was all ready for harvesting, He intentionally omitted the minor detail that giants were occupying the land. God leaves out information when He gives us instructions because that information is not an issue for Him. He does not expect it to be an issue for us either. The devil employs giants to resist you, intimidate and frustrate you, and steal the

The Enemy Of 'NOW'

promises of God from your life. There are all kinds of giants: fear, insecurity, inferiority, sickness, debt, depression, worry, stress, family problems, etc. However, whatever name you put on them, their mission is to keep you out of your Promised Land and to keep you from using your faith to push your way into success.

Procrastination is costly, and the price consistently rises. Procrastination is the fertilizer needed for difficulties to grow out of control. You will be surprised at how much is lost and irretrievable due to you dragging your feet. Procrastination is the layaway of success. Therefore, your success will always be on hold.

People who delay paying bills on time are making companies richer by the day because of the untold billions of dollars spent annually on late fees. Have you ever been late to buy an airline ticket because you procrastinated? How much more did your trip cost you? There is a difference between being late and being too late. Late in your decision may cost you more money; however, being too late can cost you everything. Don't let your alarm clock be a device that wakes you up just in time for you to go back to sleep! The hardest thief to identify and catch is the one who likes to hide in tomorrow.

Would you like to reduce what procrastination is probably stealing from you? Whatever you think about doing, do it NOW! Someday is not a day of the week.

> "Yesterday is a canceled check. Tomorrow is a promissory note. Today is the only cash you have, so spend it wisely."   ~Kim Lyons.

CHAPTER TWO

THE IMPORTANCE OF FINANCIAL LITERACY

Many people claim to receive advice, but only the wise profit from it. ~ Dr. Mikel A Brown

CHAPTER TWO

THE IMPORTANCE OF FINANCIAL LITERACY

SOMEONE ASKED ME, "WHY DO YOU teach about money and business so much?" The primary reason is that too many people do not have enough money, and too many people in business do not know how to run a business efficiently. If you do not have enough money to pay your monthly obligations, or you have just enough to pay your bills and no more, this makes you a perfect candidate to learn about finances. What oxygen is to each breath, so is money to live.

Listen to me; even if you have a quality job earning a six-figure income, you need to learn how to manage your money. Often, a high-paying job comes with first-class tastes in jewelry, clothes and cars. Therefore, when you consider your expenses, the money you make can equate to little or nothing.

According to the Jumpstart Coalition for Personal Financial Literacy, the average student who graduates from

The Importance Of Financial Literacy

high school lacks basic skills in personal money management. Many potential graduates need help balancing a checkbook and need help understanding the basic concepts of earning, spending, saving and investing. This is a travesty! As a result, many young people fail miserably in managing their first credit experience and go on to establish dreadful financial habits. Struggling through the consequences of poor decisions made from the lack of knowledge, they are left to learn by trial and error.

There is a reason so many people are living in financial straits and struggling to find their way out of the prison of debt. One of the reasons is that many people have subconsciously learned the fine art of how to spend money but have yet to be programmed to invest it. Now listen, my aim is not to impress you with my knowledge base concerning money but to impress upon you the importance of why you should endeavor to break free from disruptive financial habits. Below, I have listed seven perpetual reasons people have learned and adopted toxic and unproductive financial habits.

1. We are taught the basic concepts of working for money, not how to get money to work for us.

2. We are taught how to get a job, not how to own a business.

3. We are taught how to count our money, not how to multiply it.

4. We are often instructed to save money rather than invest it.

5. We are shown how to spend money, not how to use it as leverage.

6. We are taught the basic fear of how money can control people, but we lack the knowledge of how to control our money.

7. We are prepared to borrow to live our dreams instead of using our imaginations to avoid borrowing.

When we are involuntarily taught and shown how to work for money, we are indoctrinated into modern-day slavery. Therefore, we end up living the lifestyle of the poor and unknown. Or, we're caught somewhere in between, not poor but far from rich, and certainly not famous. We yearn for the status of importance that money brings. We've seen enough rich people treated with respect and admiration and want a piece of that for ourselves.

WHAT DOES THE BIBLE SAY ABOUT DEBT?

Proverbs 22:7 "The rich rules over the poor, And the borrower becomes the lender's slave."

Psalm 109:11 "Let the creditor seize all that he [the wicked] has; and let strangers plunder the product of his hand."

Psalm 37:21 "The wicked borrows and does not pay back, but the righteous is gracious and gives."

GIVING

1 John 3:17 "But whoever has the world's goods, and beholds his brother in need and closes his heart against him, how does the love of God abide in him?"

1 Corinthians 13:3 "If I give all my possessions to feed the poor... but do not have love, it profits me nothing."

2 Corinthians 9:7 "God loves a cheerful giver…"

1 Timothy 5:4 "If any widow has children or grandchildren, let them first learn to practice piety in regard to their own family, and to make some return to their parents."

Proverbs 21:20 TLB "The wise man saves for the future, but the foolish man spends whatever he gets."

CO-SIGNING

Proverbs 11:15 "He that is surety for a stranger shall smart for it: and he that hateth suretyship is sure."

Proverbs 17:18 "A man void of understanding

striketh hands, and becometh surety in the presence of his friend."

There is so much to know about money. Money is a powerful tool that can do amazing things for you. Money is a big part of life, and properly managing it doesn't have to be stressful. As with any relationship, it's essential to get to know it. You can always save money and make more of it through intelligent financial choices to invest it and by using your hard-earned money wisely.

You aren't controlling your money if you don't know where your money is going. You must plan, budget, and track your spending. Here is where financial literacy is born. Financial literacy is not just about knowing your credit score but making intelligent financial decisions that can make you feel confident and secure.

In today's economy, being financially literate is more important than ever. Do not let money make your life miserable. It's only money. I have come through my share of financial struggles. Learn how to manage your finances with the tips and guidelines in this book that helped me. Thank God I learned these principles early in life, but not too early. I was in my late 20s when I bought into these principles—and believe me, they work.

Financial literacy is not a luxury. It is an opportunity for all of us to take control of our money, achieve financial independence, and spend smarter. It is the key to unlocking every goal you've ever had. Teach your children about finances. It's never too early, and there is always time. The sooner you begin to learn about money, the better.

Don't let the lack of financial understanding get in the way of your goals. Learn how to manage money effectively and start investing and building a savings account today!

CHAPTER THREE

THE COST TO BE THE BOSS

The temperament of a successful entrepreneur is one of tenacity and determination. ~ Dr. Mikel A Brown

CHAPTER THREE

THE COST TO BE A BOSS

DO YOU HAVE WHAT IT TAKES to be a boss? Do you possess the skills to meet the prerequisites of an entrepreneur?

Starting a new business is both exciting and rewarding, but it is also full of challenges. One should not underestimate the level of commitment necessary. Setting up your own business requires your total dedication and nothing less. Can you employ your time, energy, money, skills and knowledge, with no sure promise that you will succeed?

THE REQUIREMENTS OF A SUCCESSFUL BUSINESS

The success of your business depends on your mindset, attitude and skills. You must be honest about various issues your knowledge, financial status, and the personal qualities you will bring to your new business. Research has shown that successful business people commonly possess specific attributes. Moreover, these qualities are paramount to success and longevity in business. A successful entrepreneur will have the following key characteristics:

1. Self-determination - A belief that results come from your actions rather than external factors or other people's actions.

2. Initiative - The ability to be resourceful and proactive instead of adopting a passive "wait and see" approach.

3. Commitment - The dedication and willingness to make personal sacrifices. (Using the money you may have allocated for other things and losing your leisure time because of long hours.)

4. Self-confidence - A passionate belief about yourself, your product or services, and your ability to succeed.

5. Being a self-starter - Means working independently, taking the initiative, and developing your ideas.

6. Perseverance - The ability to continue despite setbacks, financial insecurity, and risk exposure.

These are just a few necessary qualities. These qualities, coupled with your overall judgment, which is the ability to be open-minded when taking advice from experts in your field while bearing in mind your intentions for the business, are also needed. If you do not have what it takes to own your own business, starting a business without these qualities may take all you own.

THE NATURE OF AN ENTREPRENEUR

Starting a business is easy; staying in business is a different story. All too often, those with lofty dreams are great starters but lousy finishers. You will need tools and skills to start your business and specific qualities to help you stay in business. The same is valid for relationships. In the dating phase, couples go above and beyond to conquer the hearts of their significant others. Once those couples have solidified their relationships through marriage, they often put those efforts on the back burner. Staying in business, like staying in a relationship, requires constant effort. Success in the long term will require you to grow continually and learn. The temperament of a successful entrepreneur is one of tenacity and determination. You must be willing to fight through tough times instead of throwing in the towel when things get complicated. When life's financial and personal storms come to test the resolve of your character and business, you will remain intact with your company.

THE BUSINESS INDUSTRY STANDARD ASSESSMENT

As you begin, start by assessing your skills and knowledge of the business you are pursuing. This information will help you gauge whether you need training or to draw from outside support through delegation, recruiting or outsourcing.

CORE SKILLS OF AN ENTREPRENEUR

As a business owner, you need core skills to execute your ideas and ensure your new business survives. I can speak from first-hand experience. I am the owner of five companies with over thirty full-time employees. My company's assets total several million dollars, every penny of which has been earned and appropriately allocated. In one of my companies, I have experienced losing hundreds of thousands of dollars, but I never stopped moving forward and being creative in producing other income streams. If you take my advice to heart, it can inevitably help you avoid making the mistake of going into business ill-informed and, instead, prepare you for one of the most extraordinary ventures of your life. Listed below are the core business skills necessary for successful entrepreneurship. Take some time to evaluate yourself honestly as you read the following key business proficiency topics.

- Fiscal Management - This requires financial literacy, budgeting your income, planning revenue, managing credit, and maintaining good relationships with your bank and accountant.

- Product Development - The ability to make long-term plans for product development and identify the people, materials and processes required to achieve them. To make such plans, you must know your competition and customers' needs.

- People Management Skills - This includes managing recruitment, resolving disputes, motivating staff and managing training. Good people management will help employees to work together as a well-functioning team. It would be best if you also led by example.

- Planning - The ability to assess the strengths and weaknesses of your business and plan accordingly.

- Marketing - A positive marketing approach will help you set up, oversee sales, and marketing operations, analyze markets, identify selling points for your product, and follow these through to market.

- Supplier Relationship Management - The ability to identify suppliers and positively manage those relationships.

- Sales Skills - With sales, your business can survive and grow. You need to identify potential customers and their individual needs, effectively explain your goods and services to them and convert these potential customers into clients. Taking a step further, in an over-saturated market, you must be able to distinguish your product and company so that you stand out.

Okay, so how did you do? Keep going even if, after reading these skills, you find yourself lacking a few or all. The good news is that there is always time to learn and grow! Honesty and knowing how to be accountable for your actions is what you need for continual growth.

Suppose you read these skills and feel confident, then great! However, avoid coasting off your past accomplishments and lessons. Always strive to improve and be better so you avoid stagnation and complacency. There are always new heights and depths to reach. Challenge yourself to go further!

MARKET STUDY VERIFICATION

Now that you have evaluated yourself in the scope of an entrepreneur, you can look at how you are presenting your business and product to the world through your marketing techniques. You need to research your target market and your competitors carefully. A common misconception is that entrepreneurs who fail lack sufficient funding or do not put the right team in place. In many cases, new businesses fail because they do not spend adequate time researching their business idea and its viability in the market.

There are specific criteria you can use to establish this:

- Does your product or service satisfy or create a market need?

- Can you identify potential customers?

- Is your product or service unique, distinct or superior to competitors?

- What competition will your product or service face locally, nationally and globally?

- Does your product or service comply with relevant regulations and legislation?

- Can you sell the product or service at a price that will net you sufficient profit?

Market research can be vital in answering many of these questions and increasing your chances of success. How much research you do will depend on your available time and funds. Use the poor man's marketing survey if you are low on funds. You can casually canvass the opinion of friends, talk to industry contacts and colleagues, or survey the public about whether they would use your product or service. The more information you have, the better positioned you will be to make your business idea a success.

In summary, you also need a financial commitment assessment. Securing the right financing for your new business is crucial. Keeping your new business afloat will prove extremely difficult if you decide to launch your new business without enough funding. You need to be honest about your start-up capital reserves.

I do not mean to scare you off your entrepreneurial endeavors; I want you to be informed. So, did you fare well, or is it farewell? The choice is yours.

CHAPTER FOUR

STARTING A SMALL BUSINESS

Don't just teach a man how to fish, teach him how to own the pond so others can pay him to fish. ~ Dr. Mikel A Brown

CHAPTER FOUR

STARTING A SMALL BUSINESS
Take the Guesswork Out of How to Make Money with a Small Business.

ARE YOU SECRETLY AFRAID of losing your job and being unprepared for a failing economy? Are you ready for the great opportunities that this struggling economy will produce to make you wealthy and secure? Many people have learned how to take advantage of this uncertain economy and have become financially secure. Although nothing is guaranteed, one thing is. People will continue to make money despite the financial conditions of society.

The chances of the economy slipping into another recession have risen significantly, and forecasts for economic growth and job gains over the next year have substantially decreased. It's time to stop playing the survival game. A person who lives in a country where the economy is struggling has to do more than exist; they have to make every effort to impress and thrive. To survive a brutal economy like this, you need to spend at least as much time building your business as you do to cut costs. Take an offensive stance and act.

For those who already have small businesses, making

more sales calls and developing new marketing strategies is a decent idea. However, more may be needed for some of you to increase your revenue quickly. I'm talking about refining or expanding the line-up of products or services you offer or changing how you sell them. If your circumstances are sufficiently dire, I'm talking about overhauling your entire business blueprint.

Does this sound too risky? Let me tell you something, doing nothing at all is too risky. Doing nothing gives your competitors a chance to steal your customers and momentum. Do you want to know how to boost sales in a down economy? Introduce new products or services to help your small business beat the recession in ways that cutting costs cannot. In addition, add several new lines of products with a twist and employ upselling concepts that will dazzle your least interested client. Put your thinking caps on and think BIG. Take baby steps to achieve your BIG ideas.

SIMPLE STEPS BRING BIG PROFITS

It is no secret that people like to complicate the simple things in life. People have become so comfortable with operating in chaotic disorder that simple things no longer make sense. Forget everything you've heard about why you should start a business. Whether you accept this reality or not, everyone wants to start a company to make money. Let's just cut to the chase and tell it like it is. I want to be RICH, which means having more money to do things for my family, friends and charitable organizations. Take your pick of an endless source of income or a skimpy supply of leftovers. They say that good things come to those who wait. However, what

Dream Big Start Small

comes to those who wait is usually the leftovers of those who pick the best from the bunch first. You can think of either the possibilities or the probabilities. No one will offer you more than what you desire for yourself, and nobody should want it for you more than you do.

Everyone loves a gift. An old maxim says, "Give a hungry man a fish, and you feed him for a day. Teach that hungry man how to fish, and you feed him for a lifetime." I aim to give you one of the greatest gifts of helping you become functional and productive. A perfect gift for a hungry man is not a single fish, it is the knowledge and skills to obtain as many fish as he may desire for as long as he wants. Take it—it's yours! There is simply no substitute for knowledge.

You do not need the experience of an expert to start a business. Nevertheless, like any baby learning to walk, the baby must first have the desire to walk. Every baby has an innate desire to move from lying on its back to rolling over. From there, that baby begins to sit up independently. Soon, that baby starts crawling, and eventually that baby will begin to walk. Moreover, every adult, especially those married with children, desires to increase their revenue to enable their family to enjoy life's pleasures.

My gift to you is to remove the mystique of starting and running a business and show you how the process, which is seemingly so advanced, is quite simple. You can be up and running in no time at all. Most people who want to start their businesses don't have a ton of money lying around. The common question is, "How can I get started with little or no cash?" The answer to this question is relatively simple. Let me give you some simple ideas you can use to get started on the entrepreneurial trail.

When I talk to my protégés about business, I make no assumptions that they already know everything about it. I see them as toddlers exploring the world for the first time. I think of removing little obstacles that can distract them from their original intent in the same manner that a parent, teaching their children to walk, removes anything from their path that would hinder their progression. Have you noticed that a toddler can crawl toward you on the floor and become distracted by the smallest object they see? With all their mental energy, they try to pick up the tiny thing that demands more attention than you do. Despite how big your goals are, a person can become wholly distracted by insignificant items and miss the big picture. Therefore, let me make this process as painless and simple as possible. I put together a list below of ideas I strongly believe in and have personally used. I hope you find them useful!

The *Four Fundamental Guiding Principles* for starting a business without much money are:

> 1. Do not think about renting an office, hiring staff, or any such thing that well-established companies or small businesses have in place.
>
> 2. Your first employee is you. Second, to be employed are your family members. They can do the little things

like packaging, preparing and loading your vehicle with products.

3. Do not reinvent the wheel; use the ones you have. Refrain from concerning yourself with all the particulars like attorneys, business plans, etc. You can cross that bridge when you get there.

4. Keep your expenses as close to one dollar as possible. Nothing zaps the wind out of the sail of a business like the lack of money at the very beginning. Use your money wisely. It is not about looking good; it is about making more money.

You are probably asking yourself, "Is this it?" I believe in the KISS formula. KISS is an acronym for KEEP IT SIMPLE, STUPID. You would be surprised how many wealthy business people are less bright than most think. They like to keep things simple.

In the next chapter, we will deal with the parameters of starting a business that will have you in full throttle in just minutes. Get ready to turn your ideas into cash and create a lifetime stream of income that will keep you basking in the sun.

CHAPTER FIVE

INCREASE YOUR NET WORTH THROUGH MULTIPLE STREAMS OF INCOME

If you have only one stream of income, you most likely have multiple streams of debts. ~ Dr. Mikel A Brown

CHAPTER FIVE

INCREASE YOUR NET WORTH THROUGH MULTIPLE STREAMS OF INCOME

ESTABLISHING A NEW BUSINESS concept is easy; making that business run and producing profits takes thought, time and resources. It can be exciting, rewarding and filled with challenges all at the same time. You should not underestimate the level of commitment you need; it should also not be exaggerated. The success of your business venture will depend partly on your attitude, skills and natural gut feelings.

Pay attention to the importance of commitment, perseverance, drive and resourcefulness. Reinforcement and support from family and friends can be like scaffolding and are essential. That support can go a long way toward transforming your business idea into reality. Most importantly, you must learn to encourage yourself just in case your dream is shot down by those you love. Being self-motivated will be especially helpful during the early stages because you will most likely experience some obstacles and challenges for which you did not plan.

This book portion will help you decide whether you have what it takes to set up a new business and run it effectively. My aim is not to provide you with a look at the day-to-day reality of starting a business but to give a synopsis of the skills and qualities that you will need. If you're genuinely interested in the day-to-day operations of a company, the best way to gain insight is to ask those you know, who own businesses, what you can likely expect. Now, you must be bold, engage in a little hard work, and work late hours because setting up your own business requires total commitment. If you strongly believe a business is what you want to have, pray and ask God for the strength and tenacity to see it through.

Remember, God blesses people to start businesses that help the economy and the community. God gives us the ability to produce wealth (Deuteronomy 8:18). No one has to be poor; everyone can make money. Largely, making money depends on your willingness to believe you can and must. Let's look at some of the challenges you need to consider.

PERSONAL SACRIFICE REQUIRED

You will have to give up some things you enjoy for some time because your leisure and family time will be used daily. The physical and emotional demands can take a toll on your home life, but if you're smart, you'll adequately manage your time instead of wasting it. Do not let me scare you; although starting a business is life-changing, it can also be quite rewarding. Eventually, you will find that seeing your desires come to fruition is exhilarating and like a drug. You'll have to force yourself to go to bed or relax with your family and friends.

PRESSURE ON CLOSE RELATIONSHIPS

You will need the support of your family and friends. They should be aware of the effects starting up a business will have on your life, and they must be right behind you. Their emotional backing may also need to be complemented by practical "hands-on" support. Communicating your anticipated expectations and needs before the time comes and issues arise can save you and those who will lend their help a tremendous amount of stress. Your family may be willing to do what they can to help you succeed. However, there will be instances where the support or the attitudes of those in your circle will not be conducive to your overall vision. In those instances, it is best to move on without them and find a different solution. As your company's CEO or business owner, you must be willing to make the difficult decisions necessary to bring your dream to fruition.

ISOLATION

I have learned that no man is an island; a tree needs other trees to be considered a forest. Being a boss can be a satisfying experience. However, shouldering all the responsibility for the business's success can be lonely. You need to develop a network of contacts with whom you can brainstorm. You must have someone who knows you and "no's" you in your corner. There will be those who are "yes men" wanting to ride your wave of success, bringing nothing to the table but an ego boost. It will be tempting to keep those people around; however, that will only feed your pride and will not benefit your business. It would be best if you had people who could mentor you, correct you and cause you to think outside the box of your psychological locks. I have been the sounding board for many business owners, individual contractors and pastors, for whom the sounding board has allowed the implementation of outreaches to help their communities grow and thrive.

(Success Story) I know a Christian woman in her mid-50s who wanted to start a Southern Soul Food Restaurant. The woman worked hard but had to learn how to work smarter. Cooking was her love, and she wanted people to enjoy the love of her life—soul food. So, she found a small building that had just undergone some exterior renovations and inquired about renting it. She realized she didn't have a lot of upfront cost funds, advertising money or savings to pay employees. So, she obtained the small business storefront for less than $1200 a month and decided to open her business only three days a week—Friday thru Sunday. This woman proved to be very resourceful by buying a banner big enough to hang over her door so everyone passing by would see it. The sign was up for almost two months.

When her business finally opened, she had so much unexpected business that she ran out of food. The good thing about starting small is that people are generally forgiving and patient. One day's business provides enough revenue to cover her rent and utilities. The rest is gravy. Her grandson and one other person are all she employs, which has helped make her Southern Soul Food Restaurant a success. Her business is seeing a profit in less than seven months because her overhead and operating expenses are low. This woman is also happy to report that her donations to her local church have increased considerably. Consider how her business has so quickly turned a profit. She's the cook, janitor, and owner/manager and she loves it. This kind of dedication goes a long way and always pays off!

MULTIPLE STREAMS OF INCOME

Great for those of you who already have a successful business, great! However, the work continues! The limit to what you can achieve does not exist! Some of you reading this may still need to start in business; however, your overall goal is to have multiple avenues through which you generate income. Multiple income streams provide various cash flow sources from which to pull. If for any reason, one source fails, you will have others to fall back on.

If we have learned one thing from the past couple of years, our economy is very unpredictable. Authorities can shut down everything from one day to the next, including that business you spent years building. It can happen not because of anything you have done, but because of unpredictable circumstances that blindside you. However, refrain from creating your business with the mindset that it will fail or by putting a plan B in place. That thought process accounts for failure, which will come as a result. The idea is to open the doors of possibility with different avenues for God to bless you through.

Increase Your Net Worth Through Multiple Streams Of Income

Often, people look towards the future and envision the life they wish to have only to snap back to "reality" with a sense of hopelessness because that lofty dream seems so far away. The actual reality of the situation is that it is tangible, but the rate at which you achieve it is up to you. Multiple income streams allow you to increase your overall net worth faster and live the lifestyle you have always desired. You can dedicate certain streams of income to specific things. For example, say you have a total of 3 streams of income. One stream can fund investments; one can cover any bills/expenses you may have, leaving the last one to enjoy. The lavish lifestyle you long for becomes attainable the more streams of income you have. Before you know it, you will have residual income, allowing you to do as you please while your money multiplies!

Faith is everything when stepping out and doing something you have never done. However, wisdom is the principal thing; therefore, in all your getting—get wisdom. Quotes like this one are found in the most powerful book of all time, the Bible. Why sit back and settle for a wage or a job that will only give you a minimal raise even after years of service when you can decide your income? If your job is also your calling, I encourage you to not just work for a paycheck but work it as an investment.

CHAPTER SIX

TEN CREATIVE BUSINESS IDEAS YOU CAN START

Success is a systematic process and cutting corners will simply create holes to fall through. ~ Dr. Mikel Brown

CHAPTER SIX

TEN CREATIVE BUSINESS IDEAS YOU CAN START

ACHIEVING A STREET-SMART MBA in entrepreneurship is learning from those presently succeeding in business or a particular business segment. Why not go for it? Why not do all you believe God has placed in you to do? What are you afraid of? One of the reasons why most people are so sad and unfulfilled is that they have not figured out that their happiness is attached to their purpose.

One day, I asked a middle-aged woman, "When do you feel you are happiest?" To my surprise, she said when she was crocheting. I was amazed when I looked at all the creative designs she crocheted. I purchased several from her. I asked her if she had thought of selling them since it could help her with the extra income she needed. She said she had only thought of giving them away. I replied, "That sounds noble, but did you know the thing you love to do most is designed to feed you?" Therefore, your labor of love is supposed to support you financially. She later took my advice, started selling her crocheted quilts, and averaged an additional $1400 a month in income.

Life comes at you fast, and every day can be pretty challenging. Developing goals and creating ways to fulfill them can be exciting, but if your goals are unrealistic and you are experiencing a significant struggle, it may be because you are trying to jump from A to Z.

Future entrepreneurs have asked me how I predict the future. I don't. I prepare for it. Productivity relies on the right attitude, diligence and knowing how to produce a healthy environment conducive to living your dreams. You must see yourself as the next doctor, entrepreneur, author, symphony conductor, pastor, manager, teacher, etc. I am the epitome of this reality. If you want to see how far I have come, you must understand where I was.

I learned to build bridges to cross over troubled areas while continually moving in the right direction toward pursuing my goals. I had to accept that success is a systematic process and that cutting corners will always catch up to you. You can only reach your goals with plans and having a strategic way to achieve them.

If you have never attended a university or college, don't fret. A college will never give you the "in-class" experience to launch your business. Someone can easily attain a "street-taught" MBA for entrepreneurs, but it requires a willingness to adjust to on-the-job training and creative avenues to start, run or reenergize any business. Does God want you to be successful in your business endeavors? You bet He does! And abundantly so.

It is not just about where your dreams will take you; it's about where you take them. I can see where you are headed, and you will like it there. Whether your dream is to open a café or go back to school, hearing someone who believes in your dreams is the best place to start. I've lost count of the people who have told me that my books have done exactly that for them. This kind of knowledge is game-changing.

Wouldn't it be fantastic if you could count on having reliable answers for those times when your financial future is a concern? Would your perception of what is possible change if you always had the best information to help you fulfill all your dreams and goals? It probably would, and while it may seem like that thought process is far-fetched, it's not. There is a solution to every problem, whether or not it's been discovered; it gives you two options, go with the established key, or use your creativity to problem solve and create a solution! God blesses us so that we can be a blessing to others. I have been through the ups and downs of business, and I have overcome them all. I'm always working on new and different ways to help others make their businesses successful while constantly improving my own. Your success is God's passion and will for your life. Successful people have been strategically positioned along your path as a part of God's plan to help make it happen for you!

Ten Creative Business Ideas You Can Start

What is your dream business? What are you enthusiastic about doing but need to figure out how to begin? Have you ever sat on your living room couch and daydreamed about owning your own business? Statistically, 8 out of 10 people have voiced their thoughts of one day owning a business. People have thought of parlaying their idea into a franchise operation, while others have thought of starting or buying an existing business. Whatever the case, having a business can move you much quicker up the financial ladder than working for a company that will only give you a nominal wage.

Below are the businesses you can quickly start and make money with now. Money is a premium in our society, and life can become very stressful without having enough of it. Let's get right into these few business ventures I believe can be made actionable in no time.

CREATE AND SELL ONLINE:

People order things online all the time! Shopping malls have become less popular as the opportunity to shop via the internet has presented itself. So, why not get them to order from you? You can create your products and use sites like "Etsy" to sell them. You can create your online platform to sell your products, or you can even create your own Amazon store and purchase products on a wholesale market to sell by using Amazon. These are great ways to generate residual income!

SOCIAL MEDIA MANAGER/ CONTENT CREATOR:

With the rise of technology, new avenues for generating

income have also populated. Social Media Managers design and strategically post across social media websites to gain a following for certain businesses, brands or influential people. You can succeed in this field with an eye for aesthetically pleasing visuals and a creative side!

SOCIAL MEDIA INFLUENCER:

Many people have learned how to successfully gain a social media following while monetizing their own day-to-day lives! As a result, they've become very successful through paid partnerships and social media sites paying them to continue creating content! You can be a chef who teaches others how to cook, a stay-at-home mom with life hacks for other moms, an artist, a photographer, a gym enthusiast, etc.! The possibilities are endless! People have quit their jobs over ONE viral video, which became the catalyst for a career!

ADVERTISEMENTS/ GRAPHIC DESIGN:

With companies always looking for ways to advertise their businesses and services, selling ads can be very lucrative. Most people either do not have the time or don't know how to make their vision come to life. By way of YouTube University, you can teach yourself how to design advertisements through free programs like Canva.

BECOME A LOAN BROKER:

You will become a financial consultant helping businesses and people in obtaining loans.

PRINTING PRESS AFFILIATE:

You can receive a percentage of the cost of the project. It is more cost-effective for a printing press to have affiliates than a call center paying people and their benefits.

GARAGE SALE ORGANIZER:

You can make money with your garage sale, but you can make more money by becoming a professional. You can organize and run three or more weekly garage sales and make hundreds.

GIFT BASKETS & STUFF:

Gift baskets are one of the hottest productive home businesses around. Create baskets for all occasions—birthdays, anniversaries, retirements, births, Valentine's Day, graduations, etc.

TEACH A SUBJECT VIA MAIL, E-MAIL OR THE INTERNET:

People pay monthly fees to an internet company that sends them advice on losing weight, nutrition, vitamin supplements and other fields of interest. Imagine having 1,000 clients paying $9.95 every two months.

MORTGAGE CONSULTANT:

You can help people get money for mortgages they

hold. Being a middleman is not new, but being one does require diligence. Your percentage can be 4% as a cash-out consultant!

These are just a few business concept ideas you can do anytime and anywhere. The market is not as saturated as you may think, and it is ready for someone to introduce a whole new concept of making money to the marketplace. Find your niche and make your pitch. You can start one or several of these businesses and become self-sufficient. Just believe, and you will achieve. Do not fear making mistakes because no one succeeds without first experiencing failure. Get up and go at it again and again until you complete what you endeavor to do.

CHAPTER SEVEN

STEP BY STEP

Every step shows progression but to stand still is actually putting you further behind. ~ Dr. Mikel A Brown

CHAPTER SEVEN

STEP BY STEP

IF I AM CORRECT, YOU ARE THE KIND who likes to make money as quickly and painlessly as possible. You don't want to quit your day job just yet; you simply want more income to pay off your debts, save for your children's education and enjoy the pleasures of life without having to pinch pennies. Am I correct in my assessment? For this reason, you are holding my book in your hands. You are ready to leap into your future and, before long, leave your job behind.

There is no substitute for success. Action is the one principle that has a guarantee attached to it. When you apply yourself, you will supply yourself with the resources to live out your dreams and aspirations. All actual transformations are effortless. This is true because when you are pumped with information, your actions habitually bend to their source. You will realize how much you have changed once someone brings it to your attention.

Step By Step

The baby steps below, in no particular order, are geared towards effectively starting your business. Together we can transform you into a MONEY-generating machine by giving you a complete comprehensive sequence to create a successful small business. Do you feel the energy and excitement rising inside of you? Is your faith generating an "I Can" mentality that is ready to take off at any moment now? Fasten your seatbelt; we are about to lift off. Five, four, three, two, one!

STEP 1: Your home is the best workplace solution for a start-up business. You do not need a factory to create or store your product. Your kitchen, den or play area will suffice. Este Lauder began making cosmetics in her kitchen sink, and Paula Deen started in her kitchen. What's stopping you?

STEP 2: Need help getting things done? Only hire people when your profits have been realized. Use your kids and their friends when the workload is heavy, and serve pizza as an incentive. Alternatively, you can do it all yourself until you have ample money from selling your products or services to pay someone else.

STEP 3: If you need a graphic designer to help you design your flyers, packaging or advertisements, some computer programs give you the accessibility to do it yourself. Some of the programs you can learn quickly are Corel Draw, Adobe Illustrator, Canva and Quark, and you can learn anything on YouTube. A wide array of resources at your fingertips will allow you to cut costs. Teenagers are learning many of these

Dream Big Start Small

programs at school, so it is a good idea to solicit their services. You can also use your computer and printer for labels, flyers, etc.

STEP 4: Unless you have an attorney as a friend who can give you free legal advice, you might have to look elsewhere. Score.org provides free mentoring services. SCORE stands for Service Corps of Retired Executives. The name SCORE was later changed and is now called "Counselors to America's Small Business."

STEP 5: Your website is your Business Card. As you build your website, it is crucial to have legal documents on your site to protect you and your business. I know what your concern is. You are thinking, "I thought I could get around using a lawyer?" You can. Search websites with similar legal documents that fit your business scenario and modify them to suit your needs. It is as simple as that! Extensive research on your part is needed. You must be willing to put the work in to support your vision.

STEP 6: Do I need to start as a sole proprietorship, a corporation, or an LLC "a limited liability corporation"? An LLC is the best business structure, but you need to minimize costs and stress at the beginning of making your dream come true. Incorporate later when you start consistently earning money; protecting your business and personal assets will be especially important. A sole proprietorship will suffice in the meantime.

STEP 7: Before we go further into the next phase of Baby

Steps, we need to consider the accounting aspect of a business. Many people did not enjoy math in High School or college; however, that has no bearing on them when it comes to counting their money. Suddenly everyone becomes a mathematician when it comes to their income. If you have a close relative who is an accountant and is interested in helping your business by supplying free services, this would be the ideal situation. If you are out of lifelines, your best bet is to use Excel or Quick Books. Free Excel and Quick Books classes are available at your local library or Community College. As mentioned earlier, YouTube has videos that can teach you. Help is easier to find than you think!

STEP 8: Think of a name for your website that will be easy to remember and correspond with your products or services. Let's say you are selling weight loss information. A title for your site could be "droppounds.com or goodbyeweight.com." If a particular domain name is unavailable, do not pay a premium for a top-end domain name, there are plenty of good ones left. Get creative!

Blogs are another way to gain traction on your website. Your clients and potential clients can visit your site and gain insight from your writings. Blogs supply thoughts from you, the expert, on your genre or field of interest. Your blog will allow you to test out your ideas and get feedback on what people like and do not like.

Websites are vital to the success of your business. A website is essential if you are an author, a salesperson, or have a home-based business. You can get a free business website at www.wordpress.com. It won't be your domain and will read something like yourbusiness.wordpress.com. When you are ready to have your domain, register it at domain.com or godaddy.com and add this as a custom domain to your WordPress or another free resource. Although I mentioned two sources for purchasing your domain name, there are other places to do so. Google will provide you with the additional resources that are available to you with a simple search. Get more incoming links to your site by creating a Squidoo page. These rank very high in search engines, so give it a shot!

STEP 9: Create a logo with go power. A logo does not have to be a symbol of some sort. Your logo can be how you spell your business name, which can double as your logo. For instance, your company's name can be Laura's, and the font you use to present a simple word will become your logo. You do not have to hire a fancy graphic designer to create what you can do yourself.

STEP 10: Who Needs a Merchant Account anyway?
Accepting credit cards is no longer a complicated, detailed, torturous process. Today, merchant companies have realized that they are leaving a lot of money on the table by refusing the services of people who own small home-based or internet businesses. If you are going to accept credit cards when starting your business, do not trouble yourself with a

complete merchant account at first. Merchant companies are too complicated, too costly and require programming.

Do you remember KISS? Keep it simple stupid? Let's keep this simple and ensure that increasing your income is expedited. I suggest a simpler and less expensive solution like Google Checkout or PayPal. You can get all the free credit processing services available if you own a smartphone. Here are a few credit card processing devices and services you can quickly obtain by having a bank account where the processing company can deposit your money. View them at: www.squareup.com, www.phoneswipe.com, or www.paywaremobile.com. There are also other free credit card processing applications for your smartphone. Please take advantage of them and make them work for you.

STEP 11: Having a shopping cart is a good idea. The kind of shopping cart you will need depends on whether you use shopping cart software or a full-blown content management system for your website. It depends on your site's size, what content you offer, and most importantly, which is better for search marketing.

Avoid the things you do not understand and move on to simple, easy-to-understand products. If you are looking for a more professional look and a complete shopping cart at a more economical price, E-Junkie is available for only $9.99/month. It can perform your tasks until you move many products or services and need a better shopping cart system. I hope this answers your questions. If you have many physical effects, a Yahoo Store may be what you need.

STEP 12: Coaching and Training Is My Game

Starting a service business as a consultant, trainer, mentor or coach is relatively easy. There are presently no federal regulations or professional trainings required by the Federal or State Government to regulate this field. If you are an expert in your area and believe you can help others by offering your services, why not use your expertise and get paid for it simultaneously?

My professional services span several tiers of human needs. My expertise is as broad as my experience, covering everything from executive business consulting to marital counseling. If your strengths are in track and field, offer your services as a running coach. The field of mentoring, coaching or consulting is as vast as the ocean. It is a billion-dollar-a-year industry.

When offering your services as a life or business coach, developing a WordPress blog site and writing about one or more of your experiences would be wise. Collect testimonials and offer your services along with your rates. There is no limit to where it could take you; one day, you might find yourself advising the stars!

Select a domain name using your dominant keyword in it! If your keyword could be more competitive, it will rank high on the first page of Google within a month or two. A keyword is what customers type in Google's search box to find products or information. For example, if you are a life coach, people looking for one may use words like "life coach or mentor."

STEP 13: You Need Products

You must come up with a product worth selling. If you want to write and sell books, you can use an eBook template from Eben Pagan and write about your favorite subject. It would be great if you already have a couple of titles, but if you still need to, you will have to create them. Your books do not have to be a certain length; they need to contain content people want to read. Brainstorming comes in here. The key is to write about what you know, making it easy to put out the information.

Some people write e-reports and write hundreds of freelance articles. One person mentioned how he had produced an eBook in as little as a day. During a publisher's conference, I had the opportunity to meet and have dinner with Dan Poynter in Washington, D.C.. Dan Poynter is a self-publishing guru who sells hundreds of e-reports and eBooks on his site, parapublishing.com. His eBooks and e-reports can range from one page to hundreds of pages. The prices for his items range from free to hundreds of dollars. Just think, there is little overhead, no staff, and you reap tens of thousands of dollars with just a computer and your time.

A publisher is almost obsolete when it comes to writing and publishing books. A person can write a book, design the cover and obtain an ISBN and Library of Congress Number, all while uploading the finished product to Amazon or Barnes and Noble, and it will be on sale the next business day.

Many would still rather have an actual book than an electronic Nook or Kindle. If a hard copy of your book is more important to you, you can have your book self-published at a

Dream Big Start Small

Print-on-Demand printing company. The good thing about a POD is that they will only print your book once purchased, which means you have zero upfront costs for inventory.

STEP 14: Visibility
There are multiple ways you can increase your Google status or ranking. One way to accomplish this is to put a video on your website. There is a reason why a video on your site will not only increase your Google ranking but will also increase the probability of people spending more time on your site.

When people use the internet to search for a product, plain text alone will not capture their attention. Text accompanied by pictures is an improvement because the video stimulates the area of the brain that deciphers pictures. With videos added to your site, you are helping the text sink in and become more memorable. Many potential customers will seek out a video over plain text.

Even the most popular authors and internet gurus use videos. Most of these videos look self-manufactured, and they look this way because they are. Add a homemade video to your site explaining your product or services using a $40 webcam or digital camera to create educational or product videos. You can produce DVDs using iMovie for free if you use a Mac to edit your videos.

CHAPTER EIGHT

THE ENERGY DERIVED FROM DISCIPLINED THINKING

When discipline is established, success is unavoidable.
~ Dr. Mikel A Brown

CHAPTER EIGHT

THE ENERGY DERIVED FROM DISCIPLINED THINKING

STRUCTURING YOUR THOUGHTS is vital to experiencing success, power and affluence. Your ability to harness your thought life exposes your hunger for advancement. An undisciplined person is unstructured in all their ways. As you would organize the clothing hanging in your closet, so must you arrange the thoughts lingering in your mind. In essence, you must systematically orchestrate your thought processes into patterns conducive to producing a life of discipline. When establishing discipline, success is unavoidable.

You were not born as a person of discipline. However, you were born with the potential to create discipline. No child immediately obeys. There is an innate propensity toward insurrection within us all at birth. Even as adults, we are very reluctant to follow directions. If we listen to the inner voice of defiance, we will most likely end up in prison. From the crib until death, we should constantly pursue developing self-discipline. It must be taught, cultivated and rehearsed daily. Discipline is not a bad word. It is an indispensable word and imperative for your success. It demands intensity and rejects apathy. Not only is discipline interwoven into the very fabric of our society, but it is also evident in the life of every person who understands and operates within its boundaries. It is one of the essentials of a successful life.

The quintessential element of discipline is compliance. Whatever we desire in life, we must comply with the rules of that desire. For instance, if your goal is to earn a bachelor's degree in Business Management, you must be willing to comply with all the study requirements of the university you attend to accomplish your objective. Hence, the application of discipline plays a vital role in attaining your aspirations. Tens of thousands of potential college graduates enroll at some college or university but never finish their degree plan. So many people are resistant to discipline because of the level of intensity they must apply. Because people ordinarily equate discipline with the word punishment or pain, they view it as severe and fail to see the rewards of it. Discipline does not overwhelm you if you desire it; it does, however, carry the payment of consistency, which demands resistance to every thought that opposes it.

In contrast, there is a pleasurable side to discipline. Changing your outlook on this subject by redefining its meaning will change your response to its demands. Like many others, I had difficulty changing my view of this word. I was familiar with hearing the words, "no pain; no gain!" My only perception of discipline was a drill sergeant standing over me, yelling, "If you can't complete one hundred push-ups, you will get no chow tonight!" It is no wonder so many young adults are still acting out in defiance, what they were not allowed to do in their youth.

DEVELOPMENT IS PROGRESS.

I grew up loving cold cereal, especially Frosted Flakes, Fruit Loops and Trix. I could eat cold cereal for breakfast, lunch and dinner. I could not, however, understand why my mother, whose desire was for me to eat, would not allow me to eat a bowl of cereal. So, I decided that when I got older and had my own home, I would eat as much cold cereal as I wanted. It did not take a lifetime for me to fulfill this prophecy. When I moved into my first apartment at eighteen, I purchased at least five boxes of cold cereal. I was in cold cereal heaven. I can remember eating not bowls but pots of cold cereal. I was revolting against what my mother denied while growing up. I was not necessarily rebelling against my mother as much as I was rebelling against her system. She was working on the development of my body. Because she knew what was best for me, she understood that I could not physically develop appropriately without a more inclusive diet. I soon discovered what she was trying to establish in my life: disciplined eating habits. Thank God for mothers!

One word that directly correlates to the word discipline in its meaning is development. Development is another way of applying the principles of discipline to get the same results without the negative connotation. Although it is simply a play on words, it alters my negative perception of what discipline requires without lowering my level of intensity. If you associate discipline with punishment or pain, think of development instead. Development is progress. Everyone wants to progress in life, including the vagabond. So instead of associating pain with a word that can bring into your life just as much pleasure as pain, begin to see discipline as developing or refining yourself.

THE PERSON WITHOUT AN ORGANIZED SYSTEM OF THOUGHT WILL CEASELESSLY BE AT THE MERCY OF THOSE WITH ONE.

Success has very little to do with being proficient in the field you are pursuing. Many successful restaurant owners know little about how to cook or how to manage a dining facility. Their success is merely the result of their relentless pursuit of the "how to" of succeeding. Successful people understand that discipline is the key to accomplishment. Do not dismiss discipline as undesirable. One way or another, you will develop it, whether good or bad. But know this, complacency is the result of the lack of discipline and is an acquired habit as well; it will take discipline to break it. When a change does not come voluntarily from our minds, it will come involuntarily from our lack of mental concentration. Change is the only constant in development.

RESISTANCE TO PRESSURE TESTS STRENGTH.

You must push against the normality of life if you are going to ripen. Your muscles will never develop definition if you only lift weights that you are comfortable lifting. For that reason, if you are going to achieve a certain level of success, you must discipline yourself to be uncomfortable with mediocrity. The person without an organized system of thought will ceaselessly be at the mercy of those with one. If you are willing to pay the price for something, something will always be available. You can always obtain more if you only stop settling for less.

We are creatures of habit. Sometimes we construct patterns of settling. A habit is a discipline! You can reconstruct habits, but the new building of a good habit is more effortless than trying to reconstruct a bad one. Nevertheless, in either case, the development of discipline is worth it. Each individual must make a conscious decision about the life they want to live in the future. Is this too high of a price to pay for years of pleasure?

CHAPTER NINE

TRANSFORM YOUR MONEY MINDSET

Taking control of your mind is taking control of your life.
~ Dr. Mikel A Brown

CHAPTER NINE

TRANSFORM YOUR MONEY MINDSET

SOME SEE BUSINESS AS FRAUD or another way to cheat people out of their hard-earned money. Yet, these same people go to work for eight hours a day, five days a week, and work less time than what shows on their timecards. How they feel about wealthy entrepreneurs is simply a reflection of how they cheat their bosses. Employees will curse the payroll clerk for being even a dollar short of their pay, knowing they did not entirely work all their hours.

DON'T WORK FOR MONEY

Most people who work for money are slaves to their jobs. They do not love what they do but do it because they feel they have to. People whose money works for them control their fate and master their time. Money is like a mirror. An assessment of how you manage your finances reflects you.

MONEY IS BOTH A SYMBOL AND A REALITY.

Money provides choices for its possessors that would

otherwise be nonexistent or unidentifiable. What we do with money—how we use it, earn it, think about it, protect it, donate it, spend it, invest it, and preserve it—is nothing more than a representation of how we feel about ourselves inside. Your money represents your time, energy and intelligence, and you exchange these qualities for a wage. Money touches every part of our lives. It can affect our relationships, the way we go about our everyday activities, and our ability to make our dreams a reality.

MAKING MONEY IS HONORABLE

Perhaps you haven't been informed that it is okay to make money. To have a business where you perform a service or sell a product you believe in, is a respectable livelihood. A person who makes money as a thief or a con artist is a coward who is too afraid to make an honest living. People should not be penalized because they use their creativity and ingenuity to make a lot of money. It is the American way—the way of Capitalism. How much money you have is not an issue—your attitude about it is. Money is significant in our culture. In fact, in this nation, money determines how we keep score. Money may not be everything, but not having a more than adequate supply of it is a travesty. George Gallup said, "In the planning stages of this global survey, it was hoped that somewhere in the world, a nation would be found whose people are poor but happy. We didn't find such a place."

We cannot avoid talking about money while so many people worldwide have yet to learn how to manage it and desperately need it. Money is not the solution to every problem. The only problems money can solve are money problems. To live a life full of constant handouts from those who work to support their families is living off someone else's dignity.

> "Those who claim to never think of money usually need a great deal of it. I don't love money, actually, but it quiets my nerves." ~Joe Louis

DON'T PURSUE MONEY—DO WHAT YOU LOVE DOING, AND MONEY WILL COME

Find something you love to do, and you will never have to work another day. It is not a person's talent that makes them wealthy; the treasure hidden inside teaches them what to do with their talent. Many talented people have done nothing with their abilities and yet, have complained about how life is unfair compared to those who have applied themselves.

> "If you do something, you can change something; but if you do nothing, you can change nothing."
> ~ Dr. Mikel Brown

THE NEED FOR MONEY TO CIRCULATE

When it comes to life and business, you must understand that life is business. Twenty-four hours a day, even while you are sleeping, the wheels of life are constantly spinning. People are studying ways to get your money, whether legally or illegally. Money is called currency because of its current flow. Money is constantly changing hands and moving from city to city, state to state, and nation to nation. The moment money stops moving, it ceases to have any value. To make money in business, you must have some insight into business matters. You need to understand how money works to make money without having a lot of money.

CHAPTER TEN

MONEY DOESN'T PROMOTE YOU, YOUR THINKING DOES

Barrenness is a state of mind; those who indulge in it have made it a position. ~ Dr. Mikel A Brown

CHAPTER TEN

MONEY DOESN'T PROMOTE YOU, YOUR THINKING DOES

JAMES MOFFATT ONCE SAID, "A man's treatment of money is the most decisive test of his character—how he makes it and how he spends it." We must rethink how we handle our money or our money will end up handling us. Most people have a very unhealthy and warped concept about money and their management of it, which is the chief cause of why so many people are either deep in debt, in bondage to debt, and will most like die impoverished by debt. Americans have a chronic addiction to retail.

How is it possible to live in the world's wealthiest nation yet see millions of people relegated to poverty? What steps can we take to assure the American public that the dream of wealth and prosperity has not turned into a nightmare? How can those experiencing poverty and mediocrity in life be convinced they can enjoy the pie in the sky on the earth? While our nation is deeply in debt the American public is running a close second. Debt is the order of the day, and they teach us to manage debt by borrowing more money. However, embracing the knowledge about money will help you leverage debt, increase your portfolio, calculate and reduce any losses.

Have we lost sight of looking forward to more than retirement? One of the most significant losses to our country was when the American Government instituted a program for the indigent, which robbed many of their potential, creativity and productivity. Why? Because you can't dream for what is handed to you, and you don't work for what is given. Consequently, the power to imagine and create wealth became limited to a few.

Many people today firmly believe that those who are successful economically or who own businesses are people with special endowments from heaven. It's difficult for many of them to conceive that they, too, can live financially successful lives. If Robert F. Smith, Donald Trump, Jeff Bezo, David Steward, Warren Buffett and Elon Musk, to name a few, have any unique ability to make money, you better believe that that same power resides in you as well. The only difference between the "haves" and the "have-nots" is their thinking.

Have you ever thought of moving from an unenthusiastic lifestyle to a prolific and dynamic one? Can't you see yourself graduating from barrenness to a life of prolificacy? Having your life filled with increase and purpose is not a distant thought. Enjoying all that the earth has yielded forth, for those who dare to believe you can have it, is within your grasp. You can have it all. You don't have to remain financially broke or live out your years in a dead-end job offering headaches and long hours. Every person has what it takes to change their life of barrenness into a fertile dynamo of wealth, prosperity and happiness.

I cannot believe that people who are more financially successful than me are different from who I am. I once heard someone say, "It takes a special kind of person to be successful as an entrepreneur. Most people don't have what it takes." I partly agree with this statement. The person thriving as an entrepreneur is different from most people, not because they have what it takes, but because they take what they have and use it.

Barrenness is a state of mind; those who indulge in it have made it a position. People who claim not to have anything refuse to recognize the things they already innately possess. You can count your blessings, or your blessings don't count! Every person has more than they think they have. Of course, people acknowledge that they possess something, but they cannot see the abundance of those things in their custody.

Each person is full of an inherent, intrinsic value, which not even their performance, good or bad, can depreciate. Gold is still gold, and it does not change based on location. Whether you discover it in the mountains or the trash can, it is still gold. The U.S. Treasury Department can change the price of gold, but no one can determine or appreciate your worth but you. Yet even you can do a better job of determining that. You may lack the ability to do a particular thing, but it does not mean you can never learn to do it! As you learn more, you earn more. You may never have owned a mansion, but it doesn't mean you can't have one! You can do, and you can have anything life offers; if you only believe that you can. Jesus Christ said, "All things are possible to them that believe."

HOW WE THINK AND BELIEVE CREATES A CEILING FOR HOW FAR WE WILL GO.

One day I was with my children, driving around in the city where I live, and we went through this immaculate area with beautiful expensive homes. I told my children, "One day, I will buy a house in this area." I was not just speaking to encourage my children to believe it would happen someday. I was also speaking to myself that it would one day happen. My finances were horrible at that time. I could hardly pay for the apartment I was living in, but still, I believed. If I had thought and believed at that time that my present financial condition would remain the same, I would still be living in an apartment. However, two years later, I purchased a home in that area. There was nothing so spectacular about how I did it. I didn't remember what I said until my daughter reminded me.

How we think and believe creates a ceiling for how far we will go. We sabotage our success by what we choose to think and believe. Even if success approached you on a silver platter, your living conditions would be limited to your current thoughts. Let me put this statement in its most generic form: "Your wounds are self-inflicted." You can change your desert into an oasis if you will only select to substitute "I can't" with "I can" or "I will not" with "I will."

Refrain from discarding your talents and abilities because of a setback, a lack of education, or even a shortage of money in your bank account. You are more significant than these things. Learn not to speak out of your frustration. Many people think and speak their way into disaster when they encounter a problem that opposes them. Problems are not necessarily your enemy; they can work as solutions for what you need to fix.

Have you ever heard people say, "I've always wanted to be a doctor…but it requires too many years of school?" or, "I've thought about opening a sports shop…but there's too much competition?" or "I'd love to be an employer…but it's costly to have insurance, and besides, employees can be too much of a headache?"

Sound familiar? Many of us can talk ourselves out of a good idea before considering its possibilities. We have all experienced moments of inspiration and visions of the future only to discover a "but" obstructing our view. We hear self-doubt and all those negative voices saying, "You can't do it, shouldn't do it, or it's too hard to do it." If you adhere to the thoughts of "I can't," you will extinguish any hopes of moving ahead.

SOME OF YOUR CLOSEST FRIENDS WILL ONLY LAUGH AT WHAT YOU BELIEVE YOU CAN DO UNTIL THEY SEE YOU DO IT.

Fight to retain your aspirations and desires for life! Don't give in to dream killers or people who oppose your desire to get ahead. Take your future very seriously because no one else will. Some of your closest friends will only laugh at what you believe you can do until they see you do it. Then, after you accomplish your objective, they will say, "I knew you could do it!"

Money Doesn't Promote You, Your Thinking Does

Dare to stretch your mind, broaden your view, extend your vision and narrow your focus. While others are honing their sights on their difficulties and lack of income, you must target your strengths and believe in what you think is achievable. People may criticize the concept of positive thinking, but are those critics considering that thinking, whether on the positive or the negative, is still thinking? Everyone has the inherent ability to choose what thoughts should receive credence. It is the individual's choice and within their power to save or delete a thought.

Ironically, man is a slave to his thinking, yet he maintains the right to choose what thoughts he wants to ponder. Everything you do in life, everything you have ever achieved in life, and anything you plan to have in the future will be, and is, a product of your thinking. Your thinking is where it all starts, but the heart is where it ends. A Bible quote declares, "...as he thinks in his heart, so is he." So, if you want your financial condition to change, your marriage to improve, or your environment to be altered, it starts by thinking and being consumed with how you imagine those things. You don't have to believe every thought that comes into your head, but you do have to have a thought to believe.

Think about your life being fertile, consistently producing and increasing in goods. Fertility is fruitfulness and increase. Barrenness is bleakness, emptiness, unproductiveness, lack of vegetation, and impoverishment. You aren't remotely close to this definition of barrenness. You would have to be brain-dead to fall into this category. Poverty is stolen wealth. Don't settle! Don't recline! Get up and take your wealth back! Think that you can, believe that you can, and you will find yourself with all that you canned.

CHAPTER ELEVEN

A BUSINESS AFFAIR

The world is not only made out of matter, it's made out of what matters to you. ~ Dr. Mikel A Brown

CHAPTER ELEVEN

A BUSINESS AFFAIR

WHEN IT COMES TO BUSINESS, the one who has the most power is not the owner of the company; it is not the CEO (Chief Executive Officer) or CFO (Chief Financial Officer); it is not even the salesperson or the cashier who collects the payments, ultimately it is the customer. The unfortunate thing is that employees will often think THEY hold all the power. That sense of entitlement will inevitably drive customers and their money away with them. If you are in the retail, service, or restaurant industry, you are dealing with the public one hundred percent of the time. Therefore, instead of placing your emotions and pride at the forefront, your aim should always be to create a memorable experience that will drive the customer back time and time again.

I know an owner of a particular company who became upset because a customer did not like one of his products. Instead of working vehemently to appease the customer or taking the opportunity to gain feedback and improve, he told the man that everyone liked his product and that there was nothing wrong with it. The truth was that only a few people wanted his product aside from him. Moreover, I cannot, with any confidence, believe that those he said liked his creation were telling the truth. I told him it does not matter so much that you like it; it matters more if your customers want it. Remember, you are not buying your product; the customer is. You should never leverage your status as a leader to gain biased approval. Above all else, honesty will make your product the best. Although it may be hard to receive criticism regarding something you've created or a dream you firmly believe in, it could be the catalyst to something greater than you. That bit of information or unsolicited advice may challenge you but will ultimately allow you to gain further insight into what sells! Do not leave yourself with a mediocre product, that could cost you money in the long run, because sacrificing your pride is too big a sacrifice for you to make. It is written in Proverbs 12:1, "Whoever loves discipline loves knowledge, but whoever hates correction is stupid." Simply put, don't be stupid.

> "There is only one boss. The customer. And he can fire everybody in the company from the chairperson on down, simply by spending his money somewhere else." –Sam Walton

The only way to know how customers feel about your business or services is to see what you offer from their perspective. The way to see your business from their viewpoint is to ask the customers. However, let me warn you, if you have thin skin and get offended easily, don't ask. The models of many successful businesses usually include a customer satisfaction survey at the end of services rendered. They do this to ensure that customers across the board have a quality experience that will keep them coming back, give their customer base a voice and assurance that they matter, and ultimately gain feedback on how they can improve their services or products.

There are three primary responses that you will receive from the customers your business has served.

> 1. The agreeable customer: this person doesn't have the heart to tell you the whole truth, so they omit their opposing views or opinions when asked.
>
> 2. The perfect critic customer: this person will tell you precisely what is missing in your product or services and how to fix it from their perspective.
>
> 3. The hypercritical customer: this person thinks that the dollars they spend at your establishment warrant preferential treatment and a VIP experience. This customer will criticize everything from the lighting ambiance, to the most excellent server and tear apart every five-star rating you have received for your business.

All three customer responses can give you valuable information about improving your services and preparing your employees. However, remember that your job is to chew the meat, but spit out the bones. After all, you would like every customer to return and for them to continue spreading the word about your business.

The quickest way to kill a business is to give your customers the impression that their opinion doesn't matter. If the customers choose to spend their dollars at company XYZ, company XYZ better do whatever is in the best interest of their customers to compete and draw more customers to their business. Moreover, when the customer sees your efforts to conciliate with them, they will make allowances for your apparent business shortcomings and return with a friendlier attitude. Ensuring the overall experience and customer service are exceptional and offering a quality product is a guaranteed formula for success. Think about your experiences as a customer and what has caused you to be a repeat or even lifetime customer.

YOU may be your business owner, but the customer helps your business succeed. If your company has a 15-20% dissatisfaction rate, your company is hemorrhaging and is slowly dying. It behooves the owner of every business to pay attention to the vital signs of their company before they flatline and it's too late.

If you own a legitimate business with a consistent client/customer base, do whatever is necessary within the confines of your personal and business ethics so that your customers do not fire you from YOUR company.

CHAPTER TWELVE

PREGNANT WITH A BUSINESS DREAM

Many people claim to receive advice, but only the wise profit from it. ~ Dr. Mikel A Brown

CHAPTER TWELVE

PREGNANT WITH A BUSINESS DREAM

A PERSON ONCE MADE AN ODD statement to me that got me curious. She said, "I became pregnant in my dream." "Excuse me!" I replied. "That's why I started my business," she said. Everyone has a dream locked away inside their heart, waiting to escape the slumber that holds it hostage, but very few have realized their vision for one reason or another.

What is your dream? Do you love what you do, or are you doing what you love? There is a difference between the two. There is a song by the Isley Brothers that says, "If you can't be with the one you love, then love the one you're with." You must understand that to awaken the dream in you, you must be unapologetic when identifying what that dream is and what it means. If your explanation of your vision is vague, you may have more of a hope or a wish instead of a plan. It is not what the dream is that matters, it's what the dream does.

The graveyard is the wealthiest place on planet earth because six feet under, within the soil, are inventions never realized, businesses never started, discoveries never discovered, and dreams that were never allowed to breathe their benefits into the world. They remained dormant, hoping their owners would allow them to live and fulfill their purposes.

In 1992, when Jeff Bezos was Senior Vice President for the New York hedge fund D.E. Shaw, he described his dream to create a company selling books on the Internet. His boss at the time listened before offering advice to the dreamer: "That sounds like an excellent idea, but it would be an even better idea for someone who didn't already have a good job." People who are more interested in the paycheck than owning their dream will always, without question, lead you to believe that your dream is not worth the compensation you are presently receiving.

Larry Page spoke of one night in 1996 when he was only 23 years of age; he vividly dreamed about downloading the entire web onto computers. The Google co-founder and CEO said, "I grabbed a pen and started writing." He said, "I spent the middle of that night scribbling out the details and convincing myself it would work."

A dream is just as absolute as the actual thing. However, the real can only materialize with the dream. You can call it a hunch, an idea or even an epiphany. One way or another, whatever you call it, it is real. There is a powerful element within all of us called belief. When you strongly believe in something, nothing can convince you otherwise. When you experience a sudden intuitive leap of understanding, especially through an ordinary but striking occurrence, your world opens to all possibilities surrounding you. It suddenly becomes clear what your life's work should be.

Your dream is like a baby in its mother's womb, awaiting the month, week, day, minute and second it is allowed to live. And, like with the infant, once you realize your dream everyone will come around to see what was hidden inside of you. It will be available for all to see and experience. Don't be afraid of awakening your dream and living it because, in the end, it will bring you much joy—just like that baby.

Dr. Martin Luther King's "I Have a Dream" speech became the most iconic speech in the history of this nation, and it pointed toward a day when Black and White people, Jews and Gentiles, Protestants and Catholics would all sit down at the table of fellowship and live together in harmony. Was it a dream or a reality? Well, as we know it today, his vision became a reality.

In 2017, I dreamed of starting another company among the many I have created, but this one would be a children's learning and daycare facility. In my dream, I saw Noah's Ark. Some animals and children were on the Ark but were also playing outside of it. It was as plain as day when I heard the words, Bible Land. As I went in and out of my sleep, I kept hearing Bible Land. Then it dawned on me that I was to start a business to educate and nurture children. This dream gave birth to Bible Land Daycare and Learning Center, which has cared for many children we have watched grow over the years. Some people would have dismissed my dream as just that; however, the passion within me could not let the vision given to me die. Because of that, I can stand on the other side of the manifestation of that dream and be proud of the success it has brought and the lives it has impacted. I guess one CAN become pregnant in their dream!

CHAPTER THIRTEEN

FIVE DISTINCTIVE RULES THAT MAKE GOOD BUSINESS CENTS

No one goes into business to not make money. ~ Dr. Mikel A Brown

CHAPTER THIRTEEN

FIVE DISTINCTIVE RULES THAT MAKE GOOD BUSINESS CENTS

IN THIS PRESENT DAY, AS MONEY becomes easier to make while at the same time, just as easy to lose, if you have any business sense, it better make cents, or it makes no sense at all. Nobody is in business to not make money. It doesn't matter if you have a product to sell or a service to offer; everyone is in business to do well and make as much money as possible.

I have had the dubious honor of speaking to many business owners about the durability of their companies during today's critical financial times. And it is unanimous! Eighty-seven percent of them believe that despite the Feds and the U.S. government's attempts to pull the American economy out of the dumps, they can read the handwriting on the wall, and it's not good. Inflation is higher than it has been in forty years. Gas prices are higher now than they have ever been in this nation. However, these conditions have never stopped American businesspeople from thinking of ways to increase their bottom line and remain in business.

Owners of companies need to make as much sense as possible as to what will and will not work during these dreadful economic conditions, or else their companies will make no cents (money) at all. On the other hand, families all over the globe are struggling to make ends meet. New research indicates that nearly a quarter of a million people in Ireland have nothing left to live on after paying their monthly bills.

More people and businesses are struggling to make ends meet, and the demand for support services is growing as the cost of living rises. While companies are trying to remain or become solvent, banks are not helping the crisis by not lending. The simple answer to why banks aren't lending is because they do not have to. Banks, like all other businesses, are required to make profits. To answer their regulators and shareholders, banks must be profitable or cease to exist. The funny thing is that banks use their depositors' monies to increase those profits.

At the height of the COVID-19 pandemic, the Federal Government told the American public that they would issue the bulk of the government-backed stimulus package at the end of 2020, which would likely not be needed. That statement was not accurate, and unemployment rose at an alarming rate. To increase employment, you must stimulate small businesses and encourage banks to lend. The government should have this as a priority.

During Covid-19, we saw the world devastated and financially crushed by the force of business closures. Billions of dollars were still sitting in the U.S. treasure houses because many businesses did not qualify for the much needed stimulus money offered by the government. PPP loans aided many failing companies; however, the aid was too little and too late for some. Twenty-five to thirty percent of restaurants went out of business, yet some were innovative enough to stay afloat. Chick-fil-a is one of those incredible stories. This fast-food chain led the way, as other restaurants have followed their example. Even McDonald's revamped, though not to the success of Chick-fil-a. Innovation, ingenuity, and creativity are paramount to weathering the storms of economic changes.

What must be done today is that business owners and heads of families should pay close attention to markets and strongly consider how they manage and spend their money. Businesses should be aware of consumers' new spending trends and be on the cutting edge of selling more products and offering services without dramatically increasing prices. Customers will become loyal when they think that businesses are considerate of their needs.

Five things that constitute good business sense:

1. CHARACTER: Character is something you either have or are. People of preference try to make something for themselves, while a person of character works to make something of themselves and their business.

2. FORGET THE PAST: The past will always be the way it was. Stop trying to change the past. Stop looking at where you have been and start looking at where you can be. Plan for your future profits instead of going over past losses.

3. DON'T PROCRASTINATE: A procrastinator is always paying more for something they could have paid less for had they decided yesterday. Ask yourself. "If I don't take action now, what will it cost me tomorrow?"

4. KNOW YOUR BUSINESS: There is something you may have started that you promised to finish. Too many people know what they are running from, but only a few know what they are running to. Concentrate on finding your business purpose or rediscovering it, and then concentrate on fulfilling it.

5. KNOW YOUR CUSTOMERS' NEEDS: You have customers when you have what others need. Needs are easy to discover. The key to finding what your customers are looking for is in the many questions you need to ask.

If you want to get help to increase your profit margin, ask questions to potential customers. You will be surprised how they will provide you with answers on how to make them buy from you.

CHAPTER FOURTEEN

SEIZE THE MOMENT

When the present moment is ignored, there is enormous loss; and every time the present moment is seized, there is immense gain. ~ Dr. Mikel A Brown

CHAPTER FOURTEEN

SEIZE THE MOMENT

I HAVE LEARNED THAT YOU WILL make it happen if you want to make something happen bad enough, no matter how difficult the challenge or embarrassing the humiliation. Often, people want things to happen or situations to change be it personally, financially or physically. Truthfully, it's evident that some people do not want it that bad due to the lack of effort they display.

Making life purposeful is more accessible than most people think. What causes life to be challenging is when you have unrealistic expectations. Life isn't a slot machine where you can put in a coin and expect thousands. Let me make this simple for you; you get out of life what you put in. The natural frequency or automatic flow of our world always leads to deterioration. Without consistent effort and energy applied against the status quo, things will move only in one direction—toward ruin.

Faith in God changes everything and removes the boundaries from one's life.

Nothing left to itself improves by itself; instead, those things are typically subjected to deterioration. Ever since sin entered the world through Adam and Eve, it caused everything to move in reverse. Instead of the original flow of the creation of life and growth, things now move towards decay and death. The gravitational pull of death drags us from life to a slow decline until the end. Therefore, the natural enemy of life is death. I only know of one power that can stop the natural flow of deterioration in our world: the resurrection power of Christ that comes through the acceptance and belief in God's Word.

Faith in God changes everything and removes the boundaries from one's life. Limitations exist because of the natural current resulting from sin. It's natural to follow the crowd, pick up the trend, and live life in the direction of everyone else. It is natural to follow your peer group. It's natural to be financially broke with everyone else in your class. I have heard it said that a person's income is the average of their ten closest friends. If you want your income to change, get around people with no ceiling.

It is not natural to take the road less traveled or to go against the current. Choosing a difficult path with rough terrain and winding streets is not intuitive. However, the broad path traveled by many will lead to destruction, while the narrow and difficult road leads to life. Wage-paid jobs are great in number, but the higher-paid positions are few. One reason the narrow road is more advantageous is that it causes you to grow and expand by becoming a leader. Since few choose this path, you can use problem-solving skills and think outside of the norm to create solutions, while traveling on the broad road causes you to diminish and constrict because there is no need for any critical thinking. All God

Dream Big Start Small

asks you to do, is follow. Only a devoted adherence to the Word of God keeps you from moving in the same direction as everyone else. Only the Word keeps you believing while everyone else doubts. Through the lens of God's Word, we can see possibilities and solutions others simply cannot.

Living according to God's Word can break the connection to our association with poverty, troubling health conditions, and inconsistency. Being inconsistent slows and hinders our progress. It is remarkable to know that we do not have to continue to live in opposition to God's actual intent for us on earth. You can live in total harmony with God's Word and not miss a single blessing God established for you. The only stipulation is that you must believe it!

The road to creating wealth is not paved with gold but with goals.

People can achieve as much as they think and believe, but they will only accomplish what they think and believe. Adults often teach their children not to be afraid of the dark, but who teaches adults not to be scared of the light? They, too, are fearful of what they may see! Dismiss what God will do for you and narrow your sights on what God has already done for you. *1 Timothy 6:17* God has *"...given you all things richly to enjoy."* The road to creating wealth is not paved with gold but with goals. After you attain your goals, you can obtain your gold. Making money is not hard to do; get a job! However, to make money work for you is learning how to make your money make more money. Multiply!

You will find that although God has given you the ability to create wealth, His plan of prosperity is for every area of life. Jabez boldly asked God to make him prosperous, *1 Chronicles 4:10 "...Oh, that you would bless me and enlarge my territory!*

Let your hand be with me and keep me from harm so I will be free from pain." Often, people are very successful in one area of life and neglect the other areas that need help. It is God's will that you be made whole in all areas and continually progress!

A young lady once asked, "Is it wrong to want things?" "I've listened to sermons encouraging me to have hopes, dreams and goals, yet I've also heard sermons warning against greed, self-centeredness and covetousness." "Should I pray for healing if God wants me sick?" The problem resulting in our lack of asking and believing God for things is our lack of understanding God's will for us. Opportunities for wealth, and anything else pertaining to life and godliness, is God's will. My question to you is, does God want you sick? The answer is simply no. If Jabez's prayer is wrong for us to pray, then God's Word isn't true. Blessings are the will of God for you. Dr. Mike Murdock says it best, "They are incentives and rewards for acts of obedience." If you're willing and obedient, you can eat the good of the land (Isaiah).

> 3 John 1:2 "Beloved, I pray that you may prosper in all things and be in health, just as your soul prospers."

God would have to be cruel to allow you to create wealth and then blame you for enjoying it, or for Him to die on the cross to atone for your sins and healing and strike you with sickness. That doesn't make sense, even to a fool! At the very least, let's accept that God knows more about everything than we do. If you do not believe you can ask your heavenly Father for things, it is because you do not have a genuine relationship with His Son. His Son rights all our wrongs, and the devil will wrong all our rights.

1 John 5:14 NKJV "Now this is the confidence that

we have in Him, that if we ask anything according to His will, He hears us. 15 And if we know that He hears us, whatever we ask, we know that we have the petitions that we have asked of Him."

John 14:12 NKJV "Most assuredly, I say to you, he who believes in Me, the works that I do he will do also; and greater works than these he will do, because I go to My Father. 13 And whatever you ask in My name, that I will do, that the Father may be glorified in the Son. 14 If you ask anything in My name, I will do it.

There's always a high price when a person thinks so small.

You cannot ask God for too much; however, we usually ask for too little. Recognize that your world is your creation. If you truly live in God's world, you will understand that your portion is "all things" and that they are possible to those who believe. There is always a high price to pay when a person thinks small. Your stinkin' thinkin' causes you to forfeit your blessings. God is waiting to pour His blessings out on you, and you are stuck in the situation you find yourself in because that is as far as your faith goes. People who think small and live cheap will never believe in a God who thinks big and lives generously.

When you ignore the present moment, there is enormous loss; and every time the present moment is seized, there is immense gain. Life is full of challenges and opportunities for rewards, and when you achieve your dream, it makes the journey that much more pleasurable. God will give you room to repent and room to prosper. Repent, and you can prosper. No one can stop you when what you are doing is for God's glory except you. We do not need to think less of ourselves; we need to think of ourselves less. Make God's plan your goal, and you will discover no amount of gold equates to your life.

> 2 Chronicles 31:21 NKJV "And in every work that he began in the service of the house of God, in the law and in the commandment, to seek his God, he did [it] with all his heart. So, he prospered."

People only become what they want to be after first wanting to become what they want to be.

So why should a child of God who understands destiny be willing to face vulnerability, emotional ups and downs, and the risk of public and private failure? The answer is simple; they have no choice.

There is something special about the moment your intuition becomes more wondrous than your experience. The voice inside the head of a purpose-driven believer is louder than every other voice they hear. Others may doubt, others may criticize, and others may even judge, disparage and disapprove. However, the believer is not affected. Instead, they can see all those opinions for what they are; not right, not wrong, just unsolicited data. So, they sift through that data for the actual nuggets they can use. The rest they ignore. Why? They may respect the opinions of others but believe in their God-given ideas, abilities, perseverance and dedication more. As a believer, you believe in yourself and God's investment in your creation. This investment doesn't make you better than anyone else; it makes you confident in who you are. That overall belief carries weight and causes you to live your life God's way and not anyone else's.

There are no shortcuts to any place worth going, and there is no elevator to success; if you want it, you will have to take the stairs. Each step will get you higher and closer to your goal. When people tell you something cannot be done, do it anyway. If you can't do it, then it does not exist. People only become what they want to be after first wanting to become what they want to be. In other words, you can only hit your target if you know what you are aiming for. How do you kill a man's dream? You give him another one. Tunnel vision and laser focus are crucial to arriving at the success placed on the other side of your goal. You will always fail to be someone you are not, but you will always succeed at being yourself. Finding yourself is not difficult; you only have to stop being what you are not.

There are many parasitical obstacles and challenges out there looking to eat away at your confidence and self-esteem. To shield yourself against these psychological arrows of attack, you must have a defense that is both resistant to these alluring charades and prepared to defend you against these mental assaults. These seemingly insignificant thoughts are sometimes dismissed as harmless. But on the contrary, these thoughts come with names tied to them, such as discouragement, fear, anger and uncertainty. Regrettably, we all have experienced some form of intimacy with these hazardous pollutants designed to endanger our health and psyche. All these negatives can cause the best in us to defer to the worst in us, throw in the towel, and declare defeat without a defense mechanism in place.

People will only sometimes offer you opportunities; the rest of the time, you must create and take them.

Contract killers surround visionaries to try and divert them from their course, to keep them broke, keep them sick, keep their marriages in constant discord and keep them in doubt. Therefore, you must gather all your mental faculties to prepare yourself to stand up and defeat every challenge that opposes you.

I'm sure you've heard that you will always miss 100 percent of the shots you don't take or 100 percent of the questions on a test you don't answer, but I say you will fail at 100 percent of the things you never do. Success favors the audacious and the courageous. If you have never faced fear, embarrassment, disappointments or hurt, there is a good chance you have never taken any chances. A chance is nothing but an opportunity spelled differently. Again, opportunities are not always offered but instead created and taken. And please, don't give me that "I'm too old stuff!" You are old in your body when you are old in your mind. The body will begin to break down when you do nothing to keep it together.

When a child of God loves life and focuses on their destiny, they can have fun performing even the most mundane tasks. When there is a clear line of sight between what you do and where you want to go, work is no longer—work; it's an investment! Work is exciting. Work is fulfilling. Work, when it is meaningful and fulfilling, is living. That is why you do not want to gain a skill and then live a routine. Some people work to achieve a position to be comfortable and content. When you are creative, you despise the contentment an acquired skill brings. Adventurous believers detest the comfort an achievement offers. There's always more!

You will conquer the giants before you after you have conquered the giants within you.

The things I have learned have served as a stepping stool to acquiring more skills. Accomplishments are platforms for further success. When you have paid your dues and have seen what came as a result, you want to keep paying more dues. One of the reasons the military, sports coaches or self-defense instructors take you through the same regiments repeatedly is because when you find yourself in any situation, you will not have to think twice about how you will respond. It becomes muscle memory, and you will instinctively respond from your subconsciousness.

Now is the time for you to express all the hidden qualities you may be involuntarily repressing because of your inability to get past the personal struggles and battles of your past. You will only conquer the giants before you after you have conquered the giants within you. The giant killer within you is eagerly awaiting the next challenge to taunt you and what you believe, to slay it mightily. David, a shepherd boy, could not simply allow Goliath, the giant, to talk recklessly about his God and what he believed. Instead of shying away, he boldly declared from the power within him the fate the giant would soon come to know as his end. Successfully conquering the giant, David cut his head off as a symbol of total victory, ultimately getting "a head" in life.

There are things people find themselves complaining about not having enough of when it comes to succeeding in life. Yet all these things, which everyone possesses in abundance, are either squandered or mismanaged. The problem is not that people need more of these items; they poorly manage them. It amazes me how a person can find a thousand good reasons why they cannot do something and can't come up with one reason why they can. Could it be that they just don't believe it's possible?

Excuses are the voices of fear, cynicism and disappointment. You will never have enough of anything needed to achieve something when you are afraid of doing it. The excuse of not having enough time could not be further from the truth. Everyone on this planet is allotted the same 86,400 seconds per day, giving us 31,536,000 (seconds) a year deposited into our life's account. How are you spending your time? Or, how is your time spending you?

Every time you delay an opportunity, you place your life in a holding pattern.

People usually have more than enough time, but they must delegate it correctly. Then, you have people who will attempt to steal your time because they are accustomed to misusing theirs. Remember, you will waste your time always waiting on something. Waiting is not a signal for inactivity. People who wait for their ship to arrive at the dock are usually the ones who missed the first one. Every time you delay an opportunity, you place your life in a holding pattern. While you are waiting on certain things, confirmation, guidance, etc., you can still do so many things. For example, if you are an artist waiting on your big break or in the process of being signed to a record label, you can still work on perfecting your craft and becoming better. God guides us, and the Holy Spirit orders our steps, but it is impossible to move a parked car.

Consider this reality about those whose lives are in a holding pattern; they are waiting for a chance to decide when to move. Most people choose from sections A or B, and that will usually conclude their choices. On the other hand, when focused-minded people glance at columns A and B, they will discard the options presented to them and often create their own column of choices. When people have high hopes based on a wish that things will soon turn in their favor, it only indicates that they lack inspiration. Opportunities are all around you, but they are challenging to see when your concept of an opportunity is more like a handout.

Please take my advice and seek ways to ignite and unleash your inspiration. Remind yourself of what truly matters and who and what is important to you. Do not allow time to escape when you can capture vital moments of inspiration.

CHAPTER FIFTHTEEN

THE WINGS OF YOUR IMAGINATION

Imagine the possibilities. Imagination helps you to start something from nothing. ~ Dr. Mikel A Brown

CHAPTER FIFTHTEEN

THE WINGS OF YOUR IMAGINATION

Joshua 1:2 NKJV "Moses My servant is dead. Now, therefore, arise, go over this Jordan, you and all these people, to the land which I am giving to them—the children of Israel. 3 "Every place that the sole of your foot will tread upon I have given you, as I said to Moses. 4 "From the wilderness and this Lebanon as far as the great river, the River Euphrates, all the land of the Hittites, and to the Great Sea toward the going down of the sun, shall be your territory. 5 "No man shall [be] [able] [to] stand before you all the days of your life; as I was with Moses, [so] I will be with you. I will not leave you nor forsake you. 6 "Be strong and of good courage, for to this people, you shall divide as an inheritance the land which I swore to their fathers to give them. 7 "Only be strong and very (extremely, exceptionally, exceedingly) courageous, that you may observe to do according to all the law which Moses My servant commanded you; do not turn from it to the right hand or to the left, that you may prosper wherever you go. 8 "This Book of the Law shall not depart from your mouth, but you shall meditate in it day and night, that you may observe to do according to all that is written in it. For then you will make your way prosperous, and then you will have good success. 9 "Have I not commanded you? Be strong and of good courage; do not be afraid, nor be dismayed, for the Lord your God [is] with you wherever you go."

Where do you want to go? What do you want to do? How much do you want to achieve? You can answer this by deciding what you believe you can do. It is not how good you are at doing something but how good you want to be. Who can stop you from going where you want to go? And what or who can stop you from achieving anything? You can achieve what you can imagine.

Jesus didn't waste one frame of His imagination on images of failure. Humans see things physically with their eyes or through their imaginations. Without imagination, humanity would be completely limited—virtually all human progress has been born out of imagination—the ability to "see" things differently than they are. Does God have an imagination? Yes. Seeing with your imagination or vision does not mean that what you see does not exist; it simply exists in another realm. But it is real.

Romans 4:17 KJV …calleth those things which be not as though they were.

Mark 11:24 NKJV "Therefore I say to you, whatever things you ask when you pray, believe that you receive [them], and you will have [them]."

Dream Big Start Small

> 2 Corinthians 4:18 NKJV while we do not look at the things which are seen, but at the things which are not seen. For the things which are seen are temporary, but the things which are not seen are eternal.

How can you look at things which are not seen? Simple; only through your imagination. The only way humans can see the past, or the future unaided is through their imaginations. Memory uses the imagination. Whether planning or "jumping to conclusions," much of our thinking involves using our imaginations. Both fear and faith operate in the realm of the imagination. Many sports psychologists teach athletes about the power of the imagination, and top athletes successfully use their imaginations when training. Vividly imagining performing a successful action seems more effective in training than physically doing it. The same goes for negatively imagining a future situation. The moment you focus on the failure and even see yourself failing, you sentence yourself to do so. Before we ever take action, we first develop thoughts, which turn into those actions and later behaviors that become a part of who we are.

When we experience an event vividly in our imaginations, it is imprinted as an experience, even though we did not physically experience it. Our mind is so powerful that we can make ourselves believe an event has occurred, even though it hasn't, which has the same effect. I know how difficult this can be to accept but consider the following verse.

> Matthew 5:28 NKJV "But I say to you that whoever looks at a woman to lust for her has already committed adultery with her in his heart."

The Wings Of Your Imagination

Children have active imaginations naturally. As we grow older and become more "educated," we tend to use our imaginations less and less. It's almost as though the more we know, the less we need to discover. Over time we find different uses for our imaginations, which hinders us. We use our imaginations negatively by worrying and creating worst-case scenarios. To worry is a terrible use of such a powerful gift. Instead, based on God's Word, we should positively use that same process to propel us closer to His purpose.

Television would be a great tool to inform the public if people didn't use it to steer us into the way they want us to think. Television puts images in your mind without you ever having to employ the use of your imagination. Reading a book, on the other hand, increases your vocabulary and causes you to paint vivid images of the characters and stories told by way of your imagination. Reading a book is always better than watching a movie about it. It is such a beautiful thing to understand the purpose of your imagination and use it accordingly. When your creativity is locked up by fear, the only solution is to read God's word. In it, you will discover the only prison that truly exists is the one your imagination creates.

We all have two sets of eyes: an inward pair and an outward pair. The sight of both sets of eyes determines our thoughts and responses. When you are unconsciously powered more by what you see physically (in the natural), it can trigger what you believe inwardly. If you are led by what you see spiritually (the eyes of your heart), it initiates how you see things physically.

Ephesians 1:18 NKJV the eyes of your understanding being enlightened; that you may know what is the hope of His calling, what are the riches of the glory of His inheritance in the saints,

The NIV translates this phrase as "eyes of your heart." The NEB says, "inward eyes." Jerusalem Bible says, "eyes of your mind." Understanding uses imagination but is separate from it. Your understanding is not your imagination, but imagination can help you to understand something.

Acts 26:18 NKJV "to open their eyes and to turn them from darkness to light, and from the power of Satan to God, that they may receive forgiveness of sins and an inheritance among those who are sanctified by faith in Me."

John 12:40 NKJV "He has blinded their eyes and hardened their heart, lest they should see with their eyes and understand with their heart, lest they should turn so that I should heal them."

2 Corinthians 4:4 NKJV "whose minds the god of this age has blinded, who do not believe, lest the light of the gospel of the glory of Christ, who is the image of God, should shine on them."

Indeed, we must interpret this in a figurative sense. God had not physically blinded their eyes. Therefore, this must speak of not being able to understand through their imaginations.

You may face defeat, but you do not have to be defeated. You may meet failure, but it doesn't mean you are a failure. Every time you fail, you can stay on the ground in the shame and guilt of your mistakes or get up with a lesson learned and be one step closer to success. Opportunity is the new day of the week. Therefore, today is another opportunity. Don't stop to watch the clock, do what the clock does—keep moving. If you are looking for guidelines for doing something correctly, do not ignore your failures because those are signs of what not to do. The secret to getting ahead is getting started; the secret to going higher is to build a staircase from the obstacles you overcome.

Establish the habit of doing the difficult things while they are easy and doing the big things while they are small. Accomplishing the journey of a thousand miles is achieved by constantly taking one step at a time. The art of the start holds so much weight. The moment you set in motion the first step toward your goal, you become one step closer. How do you eat an elephant? One bite at a time. By doing your part, before you know it, you will look up one day and be in the manifestation of that for which you trusted and believed God!

No one can stop me but me. If that happens, it will not be because I can't do something; it will be because I believe I can't do it. It sounds so cliché at this point, but the statement is true, the only competition you have, is yourself. Constantly challenge your mentality to make room for growth. Issues arise and become a problem because we label them as such. They are not what they are until you name them what they are. The moment you do is the moment they become.

Situations become problematic because the moment you imagine them to be a problem, the pertaining issues gain the strength to become your nemesis. You will be buying into the thoughts designed to stop you from succeeding. I appreciate LeBron James' statement when asked how he feels about being the underdog. His reply was, "I will never be an underdog." I don't consider his response as being cocky but more a display of confidence. I finally woke up to the reality of what he was saying, which in essence, was no one could stop him but himself. Likewise, God placed too much in you to be an underdog.

> John 14:30 NKJV "I will no longer talk much with you, for the ruler of this world is coming, and he has nothing in Me."

Jesus was saying, "I don't imagine the devil to be a problem, but rather a solution to God's plan." In other words, if I imagine the ruler of this world to be more powerful than me, that makes it so for me. What others may label a problem for them doesn't have to be a problem for you. For this reason, some people can withstand more pressure than others. They see things differently.

> 1 Timothy 4:15 NKJV "Meditate on these things; give yourself entirely to them, that your progress may be evident to all."

Imagination is a crucial part of meditation. We should meditate on God's Word and allow our imagination to affect our future actions. For a person to change, their thinking has to change first.

Using the imagination has received a bad reputation

lately among certain Christian circles. Since some cults and new age groups have embraced using the imagination, some Christians think it must be wrong. You cannot determine the truth this way. After all, the devil has tried to appropriate and pervert many things that originate from God.

When I asked God if there was any scriptural support for using our imagination, I looked at Hebrews 11. As I began reading the chapter, I was shocked at what I found, even though I had read it many times before! Right in the first verse, I discovered the definition of faith as ". . . evidence of things not seen." I thought, "If it is something you can't see, it has to deal with the realm of the imagination." People would say we believe something imaginary if we can't see it. The dictionary says that to imagine means forming a mental image of something not present, a definition that closely describes the Bible's description of faith in Hebrews 11:1!

By this time, I was excited, but the chapter was only beginning. Time and again, I saw that people in this chapter had used their imaginations; they had "seen" what was not visible to others. I began to realize our faith is linked to our imaginations. The two are inseparable. Then I started understanding why the devil stirs up such a fuss over this subject, why he has inspired eastern religions to utilize the imagination: to muddy the waters and get Christians afraid that it might be wrong.

As I read of Abraham, I thought of Genesis 15:5, where God told him to "count the stars . . . So shall your descendants be." God was giving him an authentic picture of what his future would look like, which required the use of imagination on his part.

Dream Big Start Small

Those who believe the Bible know there is a reality that surrounds us that unbelieving people are unaware of. The spirit realm is where God, angels, the devil and demons are now active. However, because people are generally sight-driven, it is hard for most to realize they abide in the world of veiled reality because they are oblivious to it. How can anyone know about the spiritual realm since we cannot perceive it with our physical senses? Through the Bible, which is God's message to mankind. Whatever the Bible says or promises is not fantasy. It is reality, even though we cannot perceive it with our physical senses.

God gives us dreams and visions that unlock different parts of our brains through our imaginations. We could never perceive things in the natural which are open in the spiritual realm. When we look at Moses and the staff he had in his hand, we see God ultimately used it to perform many miracles. Moses saw his shepherd staff daily, but he had no idea of its potential until he put his faith in God and unlocked a world of miracles, signs, and wonders. When we meditate on God's Word, we tear down the walls of fear and hopelessness and believe that all things are possible! Believe it, imagine it, and so shall it be, by the grace of God! So be Biblical; be spiritual. Take what God has said in His Word, and imagine it as such for you!

CHAPTER SIXTEEN

DON'T SELL YOURSELF SHORT BY BEING AVERAGE

Your life will go in the direction of your most dominant thought! ~ Dr. Mikel A Brown

CHAPTER SIXTEEN

DON'T SELL YOURSELF SHORT BY BEING AVERAGE

THE AVERAGE PERSON DIES practically financially broke. You'll never be broke another day when you resist the temptation to be average. But if you do what most people do, think as most people think, and live as most people live, you will have what most people have. If the financially blind lead the financially blind, they will both fall into the ditch of poverty. Your life will go in the direction of the information you accept and believe. If it is true that your income is an average of your ten closest friends, change your company of friends and stop listening to the advice of those on your same level. Not because they are intentionally misleading you but because they are most likely giving you the wrong direction based on the same limited perspectives and experiences that you have.

Millions of people willfully go one mile but are more

than capable of going two. However, going the second mile will demand more of them than they may be willing to give. The traffic is never heavy along the extra mile because most people only do what requires minimum effort. Starting a business demands diligence and more time than you may be willing to offer. Though work requires time and effort, operating a successful business demands effort, time, and even more time. The work put in makes the extraordinary stand out from the average group.

When everyone else is standing, you have to stand out. You will start experiencing real success in life or business once you go the extra mile. There are no ceilings over your dreams; ceilings only exist upstairs in your mind. Every physical trainer will tell you that actual results cannot be experienced or will only be apparent once the pain starts. Most can easily curl 50 reps of five pounds, but if you curl fifty pounds, you will start feeling the pain after ten reps.

As Christians, we must understand that our lives—our very existence, has a purpose. God wants you healthy, wealthy, and full of life. Health, wealth, and fullness of life are your heritage, and accomplishment is your mandate. You can never reach your destiny without faith. 2 Corinthians 5:7 says, "We walk by faith not by sight." To walk in faith shows your faith is active. Faith in God makes the extra mile possible. Faith empowers your abilities. You can have the personal desire to go higher, but you need the fire to acquire the strength to fulfill your desire. Going the extra mile or doing more than required doesn't just build character; it reveals character. It shows how badly you want something or want something to happen.

The one miler is a person who will rarely start anything or volunteer to do something that stretches them out of their comfort zone. They have a regiment that keeps them out of any real challenges. However, deep inside, they want to do more than what they are doing, but they dread having to work longer hours, read more books, seek God harder, and give up their comfort ease.

Do you realize how difficult it is to break the cycle of being average? Average behavior is acceptable, and most people will never criticize you for that behavior. No one ever said it was easy to break cycles – real change takes dedication. But is something else preventing your breakthrough besides a failure to commit?

The average Christian does not move beyond the infant stage of Christianity because it requires more than a simple prayer a day. Most so-called Christians are not deliberate. You only find them praying when their problems demand greater power.

I believe, without a doubt, that most Christians want to be closer to Jesus, give more than what they give, and receive more than what they are receiving. I do not doubt that most Christians want God's financial blessings to overwhelm them. The question is, how badly do they want it? It is a temptation to give in to living a mere humble existence. The ability to fight temptation in any area is your willingness to do without whatever is tempting you. If having an average income, living in an average house, and driving an average car are enough for you, you will never go any further because you are satisfied with just enough.

Don't Sell Yourself Short By Being Average

If you want God bad enough and Him to help you with your life's assignment, you have to want it bad enough to fight and work for it, to give up your time and sleep for it. If you dream and plan for what you want, and life seems useless and worthless without it, with your faith in God, you will get it! You have to, with joy and pleasure, sweat for it, fret for it, and plan for it. You must lose all fear of the opposition. If you go after what you want with your total capacity, strength, faith, hope and confidence—you cannot and will not be denied.

> You see, to WANT something is not enough. Your motivation must be compelling to overcome the obstacles that will inevitably come your way.
> ~ Les Brown

Faith gives you inner strength and a sense of balance and perspective in life. When you don't have all you want, remember that God is all you need. Breaking the average cycle will take the strength of God in you.

You must be willing to sacrifice for a closer relationship with God. Many Christians have it in their minds that coming to Jesus produces a life void of sacrifices. This belief keeps them deceptively satisfied with doing just enough. Let's face it; if Christians want to walk in the prosperity of God, they will have to learn how to activate their faith for finances and give the way God prescribes so that they can channel money in their direction. When you spend your money without intention, it is like throwing your money into the wind. You have to target your cash to circulate; as it does, it returns to its point of origin. *Ecclesiastes 11:1 NKJV says*, *"Cast your bread upon the waters, For you will find it after many days."*

The Bible is very explicit on how to get a greater financial return. Giving activates receiving, but doing business ignites a greater return for others. We see this in *Luke 6:38 NKJV*, *"Give, and it will be given to you: good measure, pressed down, shaken together, and running over will be put into your bosom. For with the same measure that you use, it will be measured back to you."*

I usually start with this question when I conduct financial and business seminars. Can you determine how much comes back to you from a return? The answers may not surprise you because you may have the propensity to give the same answer. Almost invariably, every person responds the same way. You cannot give or do business expecting a particular return. Or they will say that God will decide every person's return based on His plan for their lives.

Now, as odd as it may seem, why would a farmer expect more or less of a harvest than what they sowed? The results will mirror the efforts. The Bible is extremely explicit on expectations when doing business or giving. To think otherwise would be to place a pacifier in your mouth, and believe that you cannot be held accountable for what degree of return you get from putting your money to work. Average people do nothing but expect something. Exceptional people will do all they can to get all they want. *2 Corinthians 9:6 "But this [I] [say]: He who sows sparingly will also reap sparingly, and he who sows bountifully will also reap bountifully."*

Being average has nothing to do with ability but everything to do with the individual's mindset. Your ability can be exceptional, but your thinking can be typical. Average people live a life of convenience because to break the cycle, they will have to be inconvenienced and do what they would typically consider too much. Your human nature is to want to know the unknown and see the unseen. However, if you could do that, you would not need faith. Faith is the ability to make the not yet as real as the already.

Whether or not to have active faith is not up for negotiation: Hebrews 11:6, *"And without faith, it is impossible to please God, because anyone who comes to him must believe that he exists and that he rewards those who earnestly seek him."*

There is no wiggle room: Without faith, you cannot please God. Regardless of what happens or why, your mission is to keep your faith and fight for it. For this to happen, a whole lot of change has to occur. We all say change is good, but you go first! Is this the way you feel about most changes in your life? You know that change can be positive and good, but change causes you to enter the unknown. Why not let someone else go first? However, God has not given options for His children to neglect their gifts. Faith empowers the believer to change without compromising their convictions. Too many of us are too fearful to live our dreams.

> 2 Timothy 1:7 NKJV "For God has not given us a spirit of fear, but of power and of love and of a sound mind."

These three significant components fortify you while you are moving toward expanding God's kingdom and living out God's determination for your life. Faith helps you not only forgive others but it helps you to forgive yourself.

> "When you forgive your faults, your mistakes will move on." ~ Les Brown

When you embrace faith in God as the only power for your life, you will stretch, and your capacity will expand.

Elisha went beyond the typical and asked Elijah for a double portion of the anointing on his life. Elisha saw himself as the eldest of Elijah's spiritual sons and, therefore, could not be denied based on his spiritual birthright.

> "We must look for ways to be an active force in our own lives. We must take charge of our destinies, design a life of substance, and truly begin to live our dreams." ~ Les Brown

WE MUST LIVE WHAT WE WERE CREATED TO BE.

CHAPTER SEVENTEEN

THE GOSPEL OF ENTREPRENEURSHIP AND CREATING WEALTH

As entrepreneurs that are driven by God's divine will, we are in an exceptionally unique position where we can use our businesses as our mission fields. ~ Dr. Mikel Brown

CHAPTER SEVENTEEN

THE GOSPEL OF ENTREPRENEURSHIP AND CREATING WEALTH

I HAVE HEARD DIFFERING VIEWS concerning the meaning of wealth and riches, and these two words are not necessarily synonymous. The context for using either depends on how you look at them. However, it doesn't matter how you define the two words. There is a common denominator between wealth and riches: money! We create wealth through management skills and gain riches by selling products and services. No matter how you get money, get as much as you can (riches) and learn to can as much as you get (wealth).

Let me clear my throat and start this chapter by clarifying one thing. I do not believe in the term Christian Business. However, I do believe in businesses that Christians own. Business is business, whether or not a believer or a sinner owns it. It is unequivocally and unadulterated business and nothing more. Business is simply an exchange of money for products and services. It cannot be a business if there is no exchange. To call a business a Christian business alienates the many people who are not Christians and locks your company out of potentially tens of thousands of dollars, if not millions of dollars, a year.

Can you imagine Hobby Lobby saying we are a Christian business? People would think they only cater to Christians, which doesn't make good business sense. It's not a good idea to shut out such a large segment of your potential market when you, a Christian, genuinely desire to reach your customer with the gospel.

Men and women affiliating with various religious organizations flood the business market. Some well-known large companies are owned by a church member or the church itself. Founded by devout Southern Baptist Truett Cathy in 1946 in Hapeville, Georgia, Chick-fil-A has since expanded to become a major American fast-food chain. Many people do not know that the Chang Family, born-again Christians, own Forever 21. Tyson Foods is a very religious company that embraces spirituality in the workplace. In-N-Out, the California-based burger chain, is also well known for citing Bible passages printed on the chain's cardboard cups, containers, and wrappers. If you've ever flown aboard Alaskan Air, you will likely get some Bible passages along with your in-flight breakfast. Texas-based grocery chain H-E-B's Vice Chairman runs a Christian retreat center. Does the name Carl Karcher ring a bell? He founded the fast food chain Carl's Jr. Company and was a committed Catholic who funded Catholic charities. Meetings at the fast food chain Carl's Jr. would start with the Pledge of Allegiance and a prayer. You may frequent many more companies and have no idea devout Christians own them.

Dream Big Start Small

Another religious organization called The Church of the Latter-day Saints and some of its members are known for owning influential companies in America. You may still find a Book of Mormon alongside the Bible if you have stayed in a Marriot Hotel room. JetBlue founder David Neeleman had a feature in a book titled "The Mormon Way of Doing Business." Let me give a small list of Mormon affiliate-owned businesses that I'm sure you have heard of. Black & Decker Corporation, SkyWest Airlines, and The Polynesian Cultural Center in Hawaii are owned and run by the Mormon Church. Deseret News and the City Creek shopping center in downtown Salt Lake City are for-profit businesses owned and run by the Corporation of the Presiding Bishop, the business division of the Church of Jesus Christ of Latter-day Saints. LDS also owns many Broadcasting, Publishing, Media, and realty companies.

You may not agree with all the doctrines of the religious organizations presented in my illustration. Although the LDS doctrine may not conform to the creeds of Christianity, my aim is not to support the views of any organization, whether Christian based or not; however, let the record show that I stand on the side of Jesus Christ and have made Him my Lord and Savior. That said, I am merely revealing this country's great business endeavors and privileges demonstrating free enterprise. All these companies are offering a service or a product that ultimately supports their religious affiliations while at the same time offering a way to help people in this nation. My point is not the religion; it is the practice of their beliefs that makes them successful in business.

Let's stop being petty about things that do nothing but distract us from our intent to create wealth so that God may establish His covenant on the earth. So, why can't you own a business and employ others who will be able to provide for their families? Business is business. What makes the business what it is, is the character and intent of the owner who operates the business. Whether you are offering a service or a product, it is the person running the company that decides the moral or immoral practices of that company. I believe there are many pastors with incredible business intellect, but they are told to stay in the pulpit and let a board run the business side of the church. This attitude insinuates that the church has a spiritual side that deals with souls and a non-spiritual side that deals with the business of finances.

How shortsighted can Christians be? There is a reason why Jesus said that the children of this world are wiser than the children of light. Christians can fight against the church down the street while losing members that go back into the world, and nothing gets done. The church is in the business of people, money, properties, counseling, and many other areas.

You cannot relegate the church to only one aspect of ministering to humanity. I know there are many opinions on this subject, but I'd like to wreck many of these ideas with one sentence. Jesus deals with every aspect of man, from healing the whole spirit, mind, and body to correcting character flaws about money, family, and business. Anytime money comes into an organization, howbeit marriage, the church, or a company, it is a business.

There are over five million churches in America and over twenty-eight million businesses in this nation, yet the least amount of the church's influence is in the marketplace. Unfortunately, the church is unaware of how to traffic the

Dream Big Start Small

business sector and, in most cases, very reluctant to engage in it.

The average time the believer spends in the business or workforce is forty-four hours a week. The marketplace is open to influence and is also a place to learn how to perform God's business. Christians need to partner with God because everything in life is about God's business. Business is not a separate initiative of God; it is all about God.

Over twenty-five hundred Scriptures deal with finances and money in the Bible, with only a little over 500 about prayer and over three about faith and love, so what does that tell you? God has never, at any time, been disinterested in the marketplace; however, His children are. Christians are so misinformed; they literally find it embarrassing for believers to believe that the God who can save their souls can also increase their wealth through labor and vocation. Your work is as sacred to God as your worship is.

God calls us to work with him in providing for people, especially the household of faith. Did you realize that the word for worship and work are the same? Pastors ought to have in-depth classes in theology concerning finances and business in the Bible, so they can be better equipped to save people's souls and bank accounts. Christians should view their work as a necessary means by which God cares for human beings and helps to make this world fluent. Neither business nor work is our salvation; it doesn't give us our worth and identity. It is a way God orchestrated for man to make money to provide for their families.

I read an article about the Eskimo people and how they have adopted over one hundred different words in their language for snow. People need to understand that language creates distinctions between things in our minds. It can also bring two ideas together.

Jewish people are taught to honor work because it is God's way for us to demonstrate our dignity and our appreciation toward God for His inherent ability in us to create wealth. The Ancient Hebrews deeply understood how faith and work come together in their lives. It shouldn't be surprising that they used the same word for work and worship.

The Hebrew word Avodah mutually means work, worship, and service. The range of usages of this Hebrew word found in Genesis 2:15 tells us that God's original intention and target purpose for humanity is that our work and worship would be a seamless way of living.

There are verses where the word Avodah means work, as in to work in the field and to do common labor. Moses, renewing the covenant with God, says in Exodus 34:21, "Six days you shall work (avodah)." Another Bible verse mentions almost the same thing in Psalm 104:23 "Then man goes out to his work (avodah), to his labor until evening."

The other meaning for this Hebrew word, avodah, means to worship, as in to worship You, O God. God told

Moses to tell Pharaoh in Exodus 8:1, "This is what the LORD says: Let my people go, so that they may worship *(avodah)* me." One of Joshua's most quoted verses is Joshua 24:15, which says, "But as for me and my household, we will serve *(avodah)* the Lord." As for me, Joshua says, I will avodah. I will work for and worship the Lord.

This is one of the most potent images recorded, so we can see that the word for working in the fields is the same word used for worshiping God. Avodah is a word picture of an integrated faith. Just imagine a life where work and worship come from the same root and foundation. So often, we think of worship as something we do on Sundays only and work as something we do Monday through Friday. Understanding this dichotomy is neither what God designed nor what he wants for our lives. Think about this for a moment; the Hebrew word Avodah on the other hand, suggests that our work can be a form of worship where we honor the Lord God and serve our neighbors.

> Colossians 3:23 NKJV "And whatever you do, do it heartily, as to the Lord and not to men, 24 knowing that from the Lord you will receive the reward of the inheritance; for you serve the Lord Christ."

Making God the Lord of your business is the sure way to success; to have the corner office if you give it to Him. What if before you make them, you take every decision to the true God-Father, and He gives you inside information about every step you should take?

Ecclesiastes 3:12 NKJV "I know that nothing [is] better for them than to rejoice, and to do good in their lives, 13 and also that every man should eat and drink and enjoy the good of all his labor--it [is] the gift of God."

Stephen Stives was an unpaid associate pastor of a small church and a handyman. He and his wife struggled financially. They used credit cards to buy groceries, gas, and other items, only to find themselves deeply in debt of over $30,000. Stephen felt they were irresponsible with money, even though they tithed faithfully. He claimed that their problem was the mismanagement of the 90%. When creditors started calling, they knew they had to look hard at their finances. So, Stephen had a fit of holy anger towards his financial situation, and he said, "Lord, if you help me get out of debt, I'll never get into debt again, and I'll be faithful with whatever you give me."

Stephen and his wife increased their giving, and he heard the Lord speak to him. "If you want $1000 a week, start tithing from the future $1000 a week." He worked with his creditors to pay down his debt and negotiated to pay less than half of what he owed them. As they reduced their debt, they increased their giving again. That's when he learned that good stewardship opens the door to good ideas that come from God.

Stephen then got an idea about building a small camper trailer. So, he made it, put it on eBay, and sold it within a day and a half. He received a request to build another one, and then another one, and Runaway Camper was born. Within three months, they sold three campers, and by the end of the year, they sold 140 campers. Today, more than 1500 people have purchased one of Stephen's trailers.

Stephen and his wife share their story with thousands about how God blessed them. They believe that if you give yourself to God and allow Him to work through you, you will experience unspeakable joy with your business and bring so much more joy to people. Work, worship, and serving is the only way to make life work for you instead of you working to make more out of life.

When you create a business idea and plan and share it with God, He can ensure you accomplish it. There's nothing like inviting God to be an equal partner in your business. I thoroughly believe Christians should be searching for ways to glorify God in every area. It should include our job performance and businesses, especially as entrepreneurs. Entrepreneurs driven by God's divine will, are in an exceptionally unique position where we can use our businesses as our mission fields. However, this does not imply that we need to shove the Bible down the throats of our employees or write Bible verses everywhere to hint that God is trying to get their attention. I'm not saying not to think of clever ways of sharing the gospel, but we also need to live out the gospel through our actions, so people can see how ordinary men and women, who believe in God, can live extraordinary lives through Christ.

> Proverbs 16:3 NKJV "Commit your works to the Lord, And your thoughts will be established."

Bible characters, such as Abraham, Isaac, and Jacob; Joseph

and his brothers, Lot, Job, Boaz, Abigail, and Nabal, King David, Solomon, Hezekiah, Zacchaeus, and Matthew, Joseph of Arimathea, The Roman Centurions, Lydia, Dorcas, Barnabas, and Philemon, all give insight into the different aspects and uses of wealth. These men and women did not just go into business for their health; it was how they fed and supported their families, provided for the poor, and created employment for others. The flip side of this coin is that they made a lot of money.

The men and women who lived in times of antiquity were no different from people living today. Men and women have always had hopes and dreams of achieving a better lifestyle. People who have dreams and believe in them usually live longer lives than people who don't. When you have a dream to live for, you are better off than a person with no dream. You will have a different kind of energy about you. Not only are you extending your life, but you are adding life to your years, making them more enjoyable. Your dream is not optional—it's necessary.

A person with a dream who does not have any 'oomph' to make it happen does not believe in their dream. It's not that they wouldn't love to fulfill their dream; they don't love it enough to surrender all of their faculties to make it happen.

What do you believe is missing when a person can't muster the energy necessary to create ways to live their dream by starting and running a business? If you don't know, I do. One of the most powerfully creative tools given to human beings is the ability to use imagination. And, yet, imagination is not the answer. Instead, it's what imagination unlocks when the right image is visible through a person's mind's eye. Let me spell it out for you, PASSION and MOTIVATION. When a person is missing the feeling of enthusiasm, interest, or a sense of commitment that causes that person to have a reason, or incentive to achieve something, they are generally missing what is commonly known as motivation.

If you have an idea or a goal, learn the art of the start. A brilliant idea or a plan requires movement. So, get up, kick yourself in the butt, and start moving. The entrepreneur within you is waiting to be unleashed, like a wild dog going after its target. You cannot live your dream until you wake up!

CHAPTER EIGHTTEEN

WHY SHOULD YOU OWN LAND AND PROPERTIES

Buy land, they're not making it anymore. ~ Mark Twain

CHAPTER EIGHTTEEN

WHY SHOULD YOU OWN LAND AND PROPERTIES

IF YOU DESIRE TO OWN A PIECE of land or a property someday, you need to know that land is an essential and valuable resource. Owning land and or properties is an investment in life. The value of land and properties goes up with time; it provides us with a haven and security. Land and property owners appreciate the value of their investments.

The land is a natural resource that, as time goes on, becomes more valuable rather than less valuable. It also has many practical uses for its owner. In addition, the price of land can increase your net worth and enable you to retire early if that is your desire. You may use your land for farming or recreation, or you may use it to plant trees and other plants that will help renew our environment. You may also lease or rent it out, which would provide high residual income.

Joshua 1:6 NKJV "Be strong and of good courage, for to this people you shall divide as an inheritance the land which I swore to their fathers to give them."

Living on the outskirts of God's perfect will, due to the ignorance of God's promises, negates opportunities for ownership of land and properties. Adam's eldest son, Cain, killed his brother Abel after a jealous fit and, as a result, went from being a settled landowner to being a vagabond. You ask, what does this have to do with me owning a home?

God's desire for your life is that you will inherit the earth. His design for your life is that you will enjoy peace and rest by owning your share of the earth. Real estate is a kingdom principle that God recognizes as the only means of producing a generational heritage.

God gave Adam the earth to rule (Genesis 1:28), He showed Abraham a land that his descendants would inherit (Genesis 13:15), and He gifted land to Joshua and Caleb because of their positive report regarding the Promised Land (Joshua 14 & 24). What does this teach? Since real estate is one of the ultimate promises of God, you are not truly wealthy until you own land. God makes this noticeably clear to us in His Word. He is in the business of the real estate. The word "real" in Spanish means king. Thus, real estate means king's estate.

In Matthew chapter 5, Jesus teaches truth-laden concepts that should comfort all believers. Read closely; verse five reveals a particular posture befitting a man seeking to gain land ownership as tangible proof of his wealth. I

Dream Big Start Small

encourage you to be aware of the following three ideas and their significance for your life.

THE POWER OF MEEKNESS

Meekness, in this case, is not to be understood in the ordinary sense of the word. The Greek New Testament translation of the word comes from the Greek word "praus," which means strength brought under control. A man who embodies meekness can exercise sound discipline in times of pressure and finds value in bringing his environment to order. Have you ever signed up for a night out with friends, knowing you would regret the impact on your bank account the next day? One of the wealthiest men in our modern world once said, "Do not save after spending; spend after saving."

Stay in control of your spending habits and keep realistic expectations of your long-term goals. If you want to purchase a home, seek guidance from a mortgage professional on how much money you will need to set aside so you can come to the table prepared when the time arrives.

Improve your credit score by paying off debt that may get in the way of qualifying for a home. The point is to forsake certain pleasures when a bigger goal is the focus. Your mindset will always influence your decisions. Learn to be meek in your approach to spending and watch God reveal to you more than you thought possible with your finances.

ADOPT AN OWNERSHIP MENTALITY

If you are a renter, how do you show honor to the property you do not own? Do you pay your rent on time? Do you disregard the rule that tells you pets are not allowed? Do you keep the space clean? The importance of stewardship cannot be compelling enough if you do not first see caring for another man's property the way God requires you to see it. Psalm 24:1 reminds us that the earth, and everything in it, belongs to God. We are stewards of this earth, which first belongs to Him. We should seek to honor God in all our ways. These ways include home ownership, our job performances, our relationships with others, etc.

Start honoring your current rental spaces if you want to own a home. Show and prove yourself to be the type of renter you would like in one of your future investment properties. If this feels like a tall order and you struggle to believe you have the discipline to rise above unpleasant habits that have become acceptable ways of living, ask the Holy Spirit to reveal to you kingdom standards for rental living honorably. Zechariah 4:10 encourages us to start somewhere; even in the humblest circumstances, you can show God you are priming to be an owner one day. Learn to be a better steward of what God gives you, so He can entrust you with more once your day of advancement comes.

LEAVE AN INHERITANCE

As believers, all we benefit from today took one man's sacrifice to acquire. Jesus paid the ultimate price for us on

Calvary so we could sit with him as joint heirs in God's kingdom. In the broad field of real estate, there is a term called "joint tenants in common," which means that two people legally own an equal share of a particular property. When you put your faith in Jesus Christ, you serve as a primary beneficiary to the will and estate of God. We become co-heirs with Christ. Whatever Jesus has, you have. Proverbs 13:22 teaches us that a good man leaves an inheritance to his children's children. According to God's stewardship standard, He expects this good man to order his affairs so that he has sufficient wealth to pass down to subsequent generations. Take a moment to ponder this powerful truth.

If owning real estate feels daunting to you, that is okay. Kingdom living is about risk-taking, not risk-free residence. However, as a kingdom financier, your investments in God's kingdom are risk-free because His promises back them. Homeownership is the gold standard for dream fulfillment. And, if owning a home is an idea you have only dreamed about to this point, you can take practical steps to change your fortunes by starting to employ the first steps in buying a home that will place home ownership within reach. Trust God and believe you will go from an unsettled renter to a stable landowner.

ABOUT THE AUTHOR

Any successful business owner knows that starting from the bottom has as much to do with success as having a vision, and Dr. Mikel Brown knows this all too well. Dr. Brown says, "Everyone starts from the bottom, and those that start from the top, are ditch diggers."

Dr. Mikel Brown has been in the financial industry for more than forty years and has established businesses from restaurants to staffing companies. He has also conducted financial and business seminars with Mark Victor Hansen the co-author of the Chicken Soup for the Soul series, Dr. Mike Murdock, as well as with other national seminar speakers. Dr. Brown is an ordained minister of over 40 years and is the senior pastor of Christian Joy Center and overseer of ECCM churches. He is the author of over 13 books to include Building Wealth from the Ground Up, Unexpected Treasures, and Turn On Your Life, just to name a few.

www.ingramcontent.com/pod-product-compliance
Lightning Source LLC
LaVergne TN
LVHW010954060325
805082LV00023B/99